VEGAN WITH BITE

VEGAN WITH BITE

Shannon Martinez

with words by Melissa Leong

Hardie Grant

BOOKS

It's time we ditched the preconceived notion of what vegan food is, or can be. Great vegan food isn't tricky or expensive. It isn't for the super rich, or for people who hate wearing shoes and smell like patchouli. *Real* vegan food is delicious. It is full of texture and flavour, as well as being a good thing for the planet.

Everyone deserves to eat well and feel good about it, no matter what your philosophy is on eating or how much money you have in the bank. And while this is technically a vegan cookbook for those on a budget, it's not just for vegans ... or those on a budget, for that matter: it is for everyone!

We know by now that even the keenest of meat eaters should be eating more vegetables, not only for the health of our bodies, but for the planet. You know that drawing you're shown at school of food portions on a plate? *This* much meat, *this* much veg, *this* much grain? Well, throw it out the window; it's changed. It has to, for all our sakes.

If you eat meat at all (I do), we need to flip this outdated idea on its head and start seeing veggies as the hero, and meat for what it really is: a luxury and a privilege for those who choose to eat it. We can't expect or afford to eat meat at almost every meal. Doing that for as long as we have has put our global meat production industry under so much strain that the real paddock-to-plate tale reads more like a horror story than a children's bedtime book.

For meat eaters reading this, I hear you. Veganism has had a bad rap over the decades, giving us THE WORST FOOD! Ugly veggie stacks, raw lasagnes, Mediterranean antipasto panini, and roast pumpkin and cashew cheese in, well, everything. Yuck! As a chef with proud Spanish heritage, I'm not a huge fan of specifically vegan restaurants because there are usually too many things missing that I love. Not meat, but flavour, texture, contrast, colour and balance.

This isn't a stab at vegan restaurants, because there should be more great ones out there ... but more a comment on the fact that we can all be better, both at home and in the restaurant world. To that end, you will not find yet another mushroom risotto recipe in this book, I promise. And if it makes you feel better about trying vegan food because these recipes come from someone who eats meat (that's me), then great! These recipes are ultimately about deliciousness, and plenty of it.

A lot of people gravitate towards veganism because it's perceived to be a healthier way to eat, but this is not a 'health cookbook'. While vegan food is technically better for you because it's built on a foundation of fruits, vegetables and whole foods, you will find no help here if you are looking to target your macros or any of that crap. This book is less about clean living and more about TASTY living, with a lower impact on the world around us. It's a health

book for the planet! Think of it less as a vegan thing and more of a guide to the way we should be eating if we want this world to survive and thrive.

We humans are a selfish bunch. We don't like change or letting go of the things we love. With that in mind, I wrote this book to find a way to give you all the things you love in your everyday food without being a total arsehole to the planet, or the animals still living on it.

This book is for voracious meat eaters. This book is for die-hard vegans. Regardless of how you've come to pick it up, you will not be preached to or indoctrinated if you continue reading.

Instead, you will find practical, easy recipes that reflect the way you already eat during the week – from high-rotation recipes to things that you can batch-prepare for easy lunches and dinners, such as spaghetti bolognese, soups, curries, stir-fries and stews. If you'd like to add a non-vegan protein to the mix (like cheese or meat), then go for it ... but think of these elements as supporting actors to the real stars of the show.

I've thrown in a few chef tips and tricks to make cooking and entertaining at home faster, easier and more impressive – no formal training required! There's also a guide to stocking your vegan kitchen and advice on how to make the most out of everything ... even scraps, because eating sustainably goes further than what's on your plate on any given day.

Most of all, this book contains a bunch of really useful basic recipes, from cakes and breads to sauces and condiments, that rival their non-vegan versions. And the best part is that it's all designed to be made easily and on the cheap.

My hope is that you take this book and use it. While it sure does look pretty, it's not just for show: I want it to become dog-eared and splattered with food, and never leave your kitchen! These recipes have made it from my home kitchen to these pages, and, with any luck, to your table. May you have as much fun cooking them as I did creating them for you.

Shannon

On cooking vegan

I shouldn't have to say this, but in an effort to appease people who don't take in everything they read, this is a vegan cookbook. What that means is that whenever I refer to non-vegan ingredients – cheese, mayonnaise, milk, chicken stock, fish sauce, etc. – I mean the vegan versions of these ingredients!

If you are new to cooking and eating in a more vegan way, here are some really useful tips to help you along.

1. There are a host of ingredients you think are vegan but aren't. I don't say this to shock you, but it does help to do a little research and be informed about what you put in your mouth in general. A lot of beer and wine, for example, isn't vegan. They are often filtered through fish scales or milk products to achieve clarity. The good news is that there's an increasing number of amazing producers who are making their products vegan, so keep an eye out.

2. On the other side of the coin, there are a heap of products you probably already use that are vegan, but you didn't know it! When something says chicken *flavoured* stock, read the packet further. Chances are it could be vegan.

3. Cheese. Vegan cheese is notoriously hard to melt because it doesn't have the same protein and fat structures as its animal-based counterparts. The tip is to use steam to help it do its best. Sealing it into a dish and allowing the trapped heat to steam it through will give you the ooey gooey result you're looking for.

4. Milk. I refuse to spell it 'mylk'. Just call it what it is, because I am not a fan of baby talk. My preference is oat, although unless I particularly specify this in a recipe, feel free to use whatever milk alternative you prefer.

5. Mock meats. You will notice that this book contains very few mentions of it. This is because I want this book to allow you to cook vegan on a budget, and mock meats can really blow it. I see mock meats the same way non-vegans should see real meat: as a luxury, instead of relying heavily on it to nourish you. Your health, the planet and your wallet will thank you. The main mock meats I have chosen to use in this book are textured vegetable protein and veggie mince, because they are the most accessible and affordable options for all.

6. Stock. As I mentioned already, it pays to read the label. There are plenty of chicken and beef *flavoured* stocks that happen to be vegan, so use them. Anything that means I can add flavour to a dish, I'm using it. And so should you.

7. Flavour amplifiers. There are a handful of products you can add to almost any savoury dish to boost flavour. Things like Vegemite, tom yum paste and mushroom XO sauce can be used for more than just their primary purpose, so don't be afraid to throw some into your next spaghetti bolognese and see how you go. The great thing about cooking is experimenting and finding what works for you.

8. Texture. A lot of vegan food is devoid of texture, which makes it boring. Just like flavour, layering *textures* adds interest and makes for a more sustainable way to love vegan food.

9. Tailor these recipes your way. This is not a vegan book just for vegans. If you have regular cheese in the fridge, or you want to sweeten something with honey or use that leftover chicken stock, feel free to. This isn't about hard-line veganism, but a practical way to integrate more plant-based foods into your diet.

10. I use a lot of fat in my recipes, and I'm here to tell you that the reason you love eating at restaurants is that the food we cook is dialled up to 11 when it comes to fat and salt. It gives food body and texture, especially where vegan food is concerned. By all means adjust these recipes to your comfort level, but if you want to cook my recipes the way I eat them, stick to the quantities on the page.

The vegan pantry

If you're looking to eat a little more vegan, or go the whole tamale, here are a host of basics that every vegan pantry, fridge and freezer should have. Just add your favourite fresh fruits and vegetables and you're good to go.

As mentioned earlier, throughout this book, when I list a product that is not traditionally vegan (such as milk, chicken stock, cheese, fish sauce or shrimp paste), I mean the vegan version. There are incredible products out there that mimic their non-vegan counterparts to the point that they are virtually impossible to tell apart, so use that to your advantage.

Tinned things
- Tomatoes
- Organic coconut milk
- Organic coconut cream
- Black beans
- Large white beans or butter beans
- Cannellini beans
- Refried beans
- Bamboo shoots
- Gravy powder
- Creamed corn
- Corn kernels
- Water chestnuts
- Chipotle in adobo sauce
- Hearts of palm

Bottles and jars
- Mustard, including hot English, German, American, seeded, habanero, jalapeño and dijon
- Tomato sauce (ketchup)
- Chunky peanut butter
- Curry pastes, especially Thai, Indian and Malaysian
- Barbecue sauce
- Tamarind paste
- Passata (puréed tomatoes)
- Golden syrup
- Agave syrup
- Coconut nectar
- Maple syrup
- Molasses, dark
- Pomegranate molasses
- Vegemite
- Promite
- Jam (apricot is my favourite)
- Gochujang (Korean red pepper paste)
- Pickled jalapeños
- Kecap manis (Indonesian sweet soy)
- Soy sauce, dark and light
- Tamari
- Fish sauce
- Mirin
- Mushroom oyster sauce
- Mushroom XO sauce (instant flavour: stir it into stews, swirl pasta through it, make it yours!)
- Liquid smoke
- Maggi seasoning sauce
- Worcestershire sauce
- Vanilla paste or extract
- Every kind of hot sauce under the sun
- Belacan

- Tom yum paste (great to add instant flavour to soups and stews)
- Doubanjiang (spicy fermented broad bean paste)
- Douchi (fermented black bean paste)

For the fridge
- Nuttelex
- White miso paste
- Milk (I prefer oat, but unless stated in a recipe go with your favourite)
- Parmesan, or your favourite cheese
- A limited amount of tofu, veggie patties and mock meats (these are expensive and I do not believe a vegan diet should lean heavily on them – consider them a luxury, not a staple)

In the freezer
- Leftover wine, frozen flat in zip-lock bags for cooking with later
- Stock
- Berries, mangoes and bananas (peel and slice the last two)
- Peas
- Edamame
- Spinach
- Pandan leaves

- Herbs (place fresh herbs in ice-cube trays, top with olive oil and freeze into blocks)
- Frozen grated coconut
- Veggie mince
- Textured vegetable protein

Oils
- Coconut
- Vegetable
- Extra-virgin olive
- Regular olive
- Rice bran
- Grapeseed
- Vegetable and olive oil spray
- Sesame
- Truffle

Rice
- Jasmine
- Basmati (brown and regular)
- Brown
- Black wild
- Bomba
- Medium-grain
- Long-grain
- Korean
- Arborio

Flours
- Plain (all-purpose)
- Wholemeal (whole-wheat)
- Chickpea (besan)
- Vital wheat gluten
- Low-gluten
- Potato
- Tapioca
- Rice
- Cornflour (cornstarch)

Vinegars et al.
- White
- White-wine
- Balsamic (a cheap one and a really good one for different uses)
- Red-wine
- Sherry
- Black (Chinkiang Chinese black vinegar and a little chilli oil is the easiest dumpling dressing there is)
- Rice
- Apple cider (the kind with the mother)
- Rice wine (shaoxing)

Packets
- Japanese golden curry
- Instant ramen noodles

- Ramen in a bowl
- Rice paper sheets
- Corn tortillas
- Flour tortillas
- Stock powders or cubes (there are some great meat-flavoured vegan versions out there these days)

Noodles (there are a heap of shelf-stable versions)
- Hokkien
- Flat rice
- Vermicelli
- Chow mein
- Udon
- Banh cuon (Vietnamese rolled rice noodle)
- Dried white Shanghai noodles

Pasta (all shapes and sizes!)
- Wholegrain (whole-wheat)
- Farro
- Regular
- Gym pasta (pretend pasta made from mung beans)
- Risoni

continued >

Dried pulses, grains, legumes and other vehicles for flavour

- Couscous
- Israeli (pearl) couscous
- Polenta
- Semolina
- Quinoa
- Oats
- Freekeh
- Moong dahl
- Chana dahl
- Red lentils
- Puy lentils
- Brown/green lentils
- Burghul (bulgur wheat)
- Popping corn (plain, not the kind that comes in a packet, smooshed with flavours)
- Kidney beans
- Mung beans
- Chickpeas
- Yellow split peas
- Green split peas
- Cannellini beans
- Desiccated (shredded) coconut

Dried mushrooms

- Porcini
- Black fungus (wood ears)
- Mixed forest
- Shiitake

Sugars (always organic where you have the choice)

- White
- Brown
- Muscovado
- Coconut
- Caster (superfine)
- Raw
- Icing (confectioners') sugar

Powders, spices, salts and seasonings

- Protein powder (essential in any vegan arsenal)
- Cocoa powder
- Agar-agar
- Dried instant yeast
- Onion powder
- Garlic powder
- Turmeric (ground)
- Celery salt (see page 180 for how to make your own)
- Cayenne powder
- Mustard powder
- Curry powder
- Chilli flakes
- Black mustard seeds
- Allspice (savoury pimento)
- Cardamom pods
- Cumin (ground and seeds)
- Coriander (ground and seeds)
- Fennel seeds
- Saffron threads
- Paprika (smoked and sweet versions, Spanish only, no exceptions)
- Sichuan peppercorns
- White peppercorns
- Black peppercorns
- Star anise
- Mixed spice (sweet and savoury)
- Garam masala
- Chinese five-spice
- Whole cloves
- Shichimi togarashi (Japanese chilli powder)
- Dried oregano (preferably in big bunches, available at most continental delis)
- Salt flakes
- Standard fine cooking salt (kosher salt)
- Rock salt
- Smoked salt
- Black salt (also known as kala namak, available at Indian grocers)
- Truffle salt
- Parmesan
- Nutritional yeast
- Vegg (vegan egg yolk)
- No Egg

Seeds and nuts

- Almonds
- Peanuts
- Walnuts
- Almonds (whole and meal)
- Pecans
- Cashews
- Pepitas (pumpkin seeds)
- Sunflower seeds
- Sesame seeds (black and white)
- Poppy seeds

BREAKFAST

AND WHY
I REALLY DON'T
LIKE IT

As a kid, breakfast with the Spanish side of my family meant a bowl of (stay with me) torn stale bread, sprinkled with sugar, topped with hot milk and a good splash of stovetop espresso. I called it 'Spanish cereal'. It might explain why I'm so highly wired as an adult ... and also why I am not a huge fan of breakfast. My ideal breakfast is going to yum cha with friends, when everyone is hungover or exhausted after a massive week. To that end, the breakfast chapter in this book is short, and doesn't contain many of the usual suspects. In my opinion, the best first meal of the day should consist of whatever cures the thing that ails you.

I love the classic version of these Middle Eastern baked eggs in spicy, rich tomato sauce. I wanted to know if I could make a vegan version that retained all the elements that make this dish great: the textures, saucy spiciness and richness. And you know what? I reckon I did it.

SERVES 4–6

SPICY TOMATO SAUCE
80 ml (2½ fl oz/⅓ cup) olive oil
1 green capsicum (bell pepper), seeded and sliced
1 red capsicum (bell pepper), seeded and sliced
1 red onion, sliced
2 garlic cloves, minced
1 bay leaf
1 tablespoon ground cumin
1 tablespoon smoked paprika
1 cinnamon stick
1 tablespoon chilli flakes, or to taste
2 teaspoons pepper
1 teaspoon ground turmeric
2 teaspoons salt
2 × 400 g (14 oz) tins diced tomatoes
¼ bunch coriander (cilantro) leaves, roughly chopped
¼ bunch flat-leaf (Italian) parsley leaves, roughly chopped
juice of ½ lemon

CORIANDER DUMPLINGS
500 g (1 lb 2 oz) fresh medium/firm tofu
1 small handful coriander (cilantro) leaves
¼ teaspoon baking powder
1 teaspoon salt
½ teaspoon pepper
2 tablespoons No Egg whisked with 2 tablespoons cold water
3 tablespoons plain (all-purpose) flour
2 tablespoons nutritional yeast
1 garlic clove, minced

To make the sauce, heat the oil in a deep saucepan over a medium heat. Add the capsicum and onion, along with a pinch of salt, and cook until beginning to soften. Add the garlic, bay leaf, spices and salt and cook, stirring, for another minute. Add the tomatoes, then reduce the heat to low and simmer the sauce for 20 minutes.

Meanwhile, to make the dumplings, place all the ingredients in a food processor and blitz until smooth and well combined. Fill a large saucepan with salted water and bring to a gentle simmer. Using two spoons, scoop the mixture and roughly quenelle, then drop into the simmering water, making sure you don't overcrowd the pan (cook them in batches if necessary). Once the dumplings float to the top, cook for 1 minute, then remove with a slotted spoon.

Add the dumplings to the sauce in a single layer and cook for another 5 minutes. Finish with the herbs and lemon juice, adjust the seasoning to taste and serve.

NOTE
The dumplings can be prepared in advance and stored, cooked or uncooked, in the fridge.

My dislike of breakfast has been well documented, but when I lived in Sydney I would go to this one place religiously to eat this dish, yes, at breakfast. I don't remember the name of the place, and sadly it has since closed, but the memory of their delicious Middle Eastern dish lives on in this cracking recipe.

SERVES 4–6

2 tablespoons extra-virgin olive oil
1 red onion, thinly sliced
4 garlic cloves, minced
400 g (14 oz) veggie mince or
  soaked textured vegetable protein
2 teaspoons cumin seeds
1 tablespoon ground coriander
½ teaspoon ground cinnamon
2 teaspoons dried mint
1 teaspoon caster (superfine) sugar
1 tablespoon tomato paste
  (concentrated purée)
2 tablespoons harissa
125 ml (4 fl oz/½ cup) beef or
  vegetable stock
juice of ½ lemon
1 tablespoon pomegranate molasses
  (optional)
1 handful flat-leaf (Italian) parsley
  leaves, chopped, plus extra to
  garnish
1 handful dill, chopped
Hummus (page 162), to serve
1 handful toasted pine nuts, pepitas
  (pumpkin seeds) or almonds
mint, to garnish

SPICED BUTTER
80 g (2¾ oz) ghee or butter
1 tablespoon baharat
½ teaspoon grated ginger
½ teaspoon salt

Heat the oil in a frying pan over a medium heat and cook the onion until it begins to soften. Add the garlic and cook for another minute, then add the mince and toss to combine. Stir in the spices, dried mint and sugar, then add the tomato paste and harissa and stir to combine.

Mix through the stock and cook until the liquid has almost completely evaporated. Finish with the lemon juice and pomegranate molasses (if using), followed by the chopped herbs. Season to taste with salt and pepper.

To make the spiced butter, melt the ghee in a small saucepan or frying pan over a medium heat. Add the baharat, ginger and salt and cook for about 30 seconds, or until fragrant. Spoon over the Turkish mince.

To serve, spread some hummus onto a plate, then pile the mince on top. Garnish with the nuts or seeds and herbs.

Okonomiyaki

It's not often you find another chef who understands and produces flavours the way you do yourself. When I first met Tamara, she had just finished cooking on one of the Sea Shepherd boats patrolling the Antarctic. The minute I met her, I offered her an apprenticeship. Four years later, not only had she become an incredible chef, but also an incredible stick and poke artist. So like a mother bird, I gently pushed her out of the nest and encouraged her to pursue her other art, and she quickly became one of Australia's best tattoo artists. This is a recipe from her, to celebrate the good old days.

This Japanese savoury pancake is a great breakfast dish. 'Okonomi' roughly translates as 'how you like it', and 'yaki' means 'fried'. This means you can throw anything you like into the batter and fry, my pretties *insert evil witch cackle*.

Place the kombu pieces and water in a small saucepan and bring to a simmer to make a simple dashi. Reduce the heat to low and leave on the heat for 10 minutes, then set aside to cool.

To make the tonkatsu sauce, combine the worcestershire, tomato sauce, sugar and fish sauce in a small bowl. Place the arrowroot in a small saucepan with 1 tablespoon of the sauce mix and whisk until smooth and well combined. Add the remaining sauce mix and simmer, whisking, over a low heat for a few minutes until the sauce has thickened slightly. Take off the heat and set aside to cool completely.

Mix together the plain and chickpea flour, salts, nutritional yeast (if using), baking powder and shichimi togarashi in a medium bowl. Pour in 250 ml (8½ fl oz/1 cup) of the cooled dashi at a time until you have a somewhat thick batter just able to be whisked easily. Coat the cabbage in the rice flour and add it to the batter, then add the daikon, half the spring onion and 1 tablespoon of the pickled ginger (if using) and mix until all the ingredients are incorporated. If you're including seafood, add it to the batter at this point and mix well.

Pour a little oil into a heavy-based saucepan to coat the bottom and warm over a medium heat. Depending on how many pancakes you want to make, scoop between 250 ml (8½ fl oz/1 cup) and 375 ml (12½ fl oz/1½ cups) of your vegetable batter into the pan to form a very thick pancake. Cook on both sides to a deep crispy brown, about 3–4 minutes, then remove and cool on paper towel to soak up any excess oil. Repeat with the remaining oil and batter.

If you are using the optional ingredients (mushroom, bacon and/or cheddar), don't cook both sides of the pancake. Instead, cook one side only, place your choice of ingredients (cheese first, then bacon and/or mushroom) on the uncooked side, then carefully flip the pancake and cook over a slightly lower heat until browned. Drain on paper towel.

Serve the pancakes warm, topped with mayonnaise, tonkatsu sauce, dried seaweed and the remaining spring onion and pickled ginger.

SERVES 4–6

3 × 5 cm (2 in) pieces of dried kombu
750 ml (25½ fl oz/3 cups) water
225 g (8 oz/1½ cups) plain (all-purpose) flour
55 g (2 oz/½ cup) besan (chickpea flour)
2 teaspoons black salt
1 teaspoon salt
2½ tablespoons nutritional yeast (optional)
1 teaspoon baking powder
2 teaspoons shichimi togarashi
450 g (1 lb/6 cups) thinly sliced very green cabbage, tossed with 1 teaspoon salt
3 tablespoons rice flour
1 small daikon, coarsely grated
4 spring onions (scallions), sliced
2 tablespoons roughly chopped pickled ginger (optional)
3 tablespoons vegetable oil
Mayonnaise (page 167), to serve
3 tablespoons dried seaweed flakes or strips, or thinly sliced nori, to serve

TONKATSU SAUCE

80 ml (2½ fl oz/⅓ cup) worcestershire sauce
80 ml (2½ fl oz/⅓ cup) tomato sauce (ketchup)
1½ tablespoons brown sugar
1 tablespoon fish sauce or 1½ tablespoons oyster sauce
¼ teaspoon arrowroot powder

OPTIONAL EXTRAS

about 200 g (7 oz) prawns (shrimp) or squid, thinly sliced
12 thin slices king oyster mushroom
12 slices bacon
12 slices cheddar

Vegan with bite

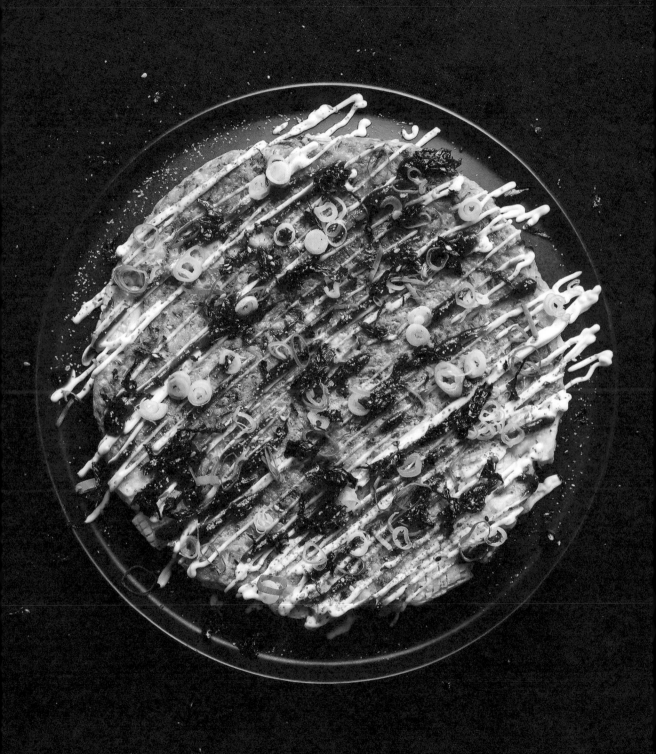

Coconut and passionfruit tapioca

If you loved Yogo (the gloopy, sunshine-yellow pudding made popular in the '80s), then this sweet, gloopy brekkie is for you.

Bring a large saucepan of water to the boil, then pour in the sago. Bring back to the boil, then reduce the heat to medium and simmer for 10 minutes, or until the pearls are almost totally translucent. Remove from the heat, cover with a lid and let stand for 5 minutes.

Pour the coconut milk and water into another saucepan, then drop in the palm sugar, kaffir lime leaves and a pinch of salt. Bring up to the boil, then reduce the heat and simmer until the sugar has melted. Remove from the heat and allow to stand.

Drain the sago in a sieve and run under cold water. Transfer to a large bowl and pour over the coconut milk mixture and passionfruit pulp. Stir well to combine, then refrigerate until cool. Make it the night before if you're organised.

SERVES 4–6

195 g (7 oz/1 cup) sago
  (tapioca) pearls
1 × 400 ml (13½ fl oz) tin
  coconut milk
500 ml (17 fl oz/2 cups) water
150 g (5½ oz) palm sugar (jaggery)
2 kaffir lime leaves
pulp from 10 passionfruit

Pandan rice pudding

For fans of dessert for breakfast, this recipe blends the comfort of a classic rice pudding with fragrant South-East Asian class. For those who haven't yet experienced it, I like to describe cooking with pandan as having all the flavour of vanilla-scented baked goods fused with the magical smell of rain falling in the jungle.

Combine all the ingredients and a pinch of salt in a medium saucepan over a high heat and bring to the boil. Reduce the heat to low and simmer gently for 30–40 minutes, stirring frequently, until the rice is soft and very creamy. Add more water or milk if it absorbs too quickly. Remove the pandan and lemongrass and serve hot or cold. You can make this the night before if you want to have it ready to go – just add a splash of water or milk and reheat if you prefer it warm. Feel free to top it with your favourite fresh or stewed fruit, shredded coconut, nuts ... whatever you like!

Pictured page 29

SERVES 4–6

150 g (5½ oz/¾ cup) jasmine rice
1 × 400 ml (13½ fl oz) tin coconut milk
250 ml (8½ fl oz/1 cup) milk, plus extra if needed
375 ml (12½ fl oz/1½ cups) water, plus extra if needed
100 g (3½ oz) palm sugar (jaggery) or other sugar
2 pandan leaves, knotted
1 × 5 cm (2 in) piece of lemongrass, bruised

Banana bread is a classic Australian on-the-run café choice, but I am not going to deny that the banana in this recipe is only there to make it socially acceptable to eat chocolate first thing in the morning.

MAKES 8–10 SLICES

3 very ripe bananas
  (approximately 250 g/9 oz)
120 g (4½ oz) butter, melted
80 ml (2½ fl oz/⅓ cup) milk
½ teaspoon apple-cider vinegar
1 teaspoon vanilla extract
180 g (6½ oz) plain
  (all-purpose) flour
3 tablespoons dark cocoa powder
1 teaspoon bicarbonate of soda
  (baking soda)
1½ teaspoons baking powder
1 teaspoon ground cinnamon
3 tablespoons caster (superfine)
  sugar
115 g (4 oz/½ cup firmly packed)
  brown sugar
90 g (3 oz/½ cup) chocolate chips
  or chunks

Preheat the oven to 180°C (350°F) and grease and line a medium loaf (bar) tin.

In a bowl, mash the bananas until smooth, then pour in the melted butter, milk, vinegar and vanilla. Stir well, then set aside.

Sift the flour, cocoa powder, bicarbonate of soda, baking powder and cinnamon into a large mixing bowl. Add the sugars and a pinch of salt and mix to combine. Create a well in the middle, then pour in the banana mixture. Using a spatula, fold the wet ingredients into the dry until just combined (you don't want to overwork the batter). Fold through half the choc chips.

Pour the batter into the prepared tin, smooth the top and sprinkle with the remaining choc chips. Bake for 40–50 minutes, or until a skewer inserted in the centre comes out clean. Remove from the oven and cool in the tin for a few minutes, then turn out onto a wire rack to cool to room temperature. Cut into thick slices and serve. Wrap leftovers in plastic wrap and store at room temperature for up to 5 days.

I could never have anticipated that this recipe would become as beloved as it has. Congee is embraced by billions of people across many Asian cultures. It's warming, savoury, and can be customised with your favourite toppings – just like porridge, only interesting. It's time the rest of the world realised how brilliant it can be to have a bowl of congee for breakfast (or any time of day, really).

SERVES 4–6

2 tablespoons vegetable oil
2 large spring onions (scallions), sliced, white and green parts separated
2 garlic cloves, minced
4 cm (1½ in) piece of ginger, peeled and cut into fine matchsticks
1 star anise
100 g (3½ oz/½ cup) jasmine rice
2 tablespoons shaoxing rice wine
1 tablespoon light soy sauce
1 litre (34 fl oz/4 cups) chicken stock
white pepper

Heat the oil in a large saucepan over a medium heat. Add the white part of the spring onion, along with the garlic and ginger, and cook until softened. Add the star anise and cook for another minute. Add the rice and stir to coat the grains, then pour in the rice wine and soy sauce and cook for 30 seconds. Add the stock and bring up to a simmer, stirring often.

Reduce the heat to low and simmer gently, stirring often to avoid sticking, for 30–45 minutes, or until the rice is very soft and beginning to fall apart. Add a splash of water if it becomes too thick – it should resemble thick porridge. Season with salt and white pepper, scatter over the green part of the spring onion and serve.

Now it's time to make this congee your own. Some of my favourite toppings are:
- thinly sliced spring onion (scallion)
- shredded iceberg lettuce
- cooked mushroom
- crispy bacon
- prawns (shrimp)
- shredded chicken
- chilli (all kinds)
- blanched greens
- blanched or grilled asparagus
- fresh herbs, especially coriander (cilantro)
- fried sausage
- fried smoked tofu
- seaweed
- corn kernels
- crispy fried shallots
- toasted sesame seeds
- Chinese pickled vegetables

Finish it with:
- a few drops of sesame oil
- chilli oil (see page 164)
- a splash of black vinegar

I've stopped inviting my vegan and vegetarian friends out to yum cha because it's near impossible to find enough variety to keep it interesting. However, I believe that everyone deserves good dumplings, and this recipe is a keeper. Throw them into noodles or a broth (or both!) for added joy.

SERVES 4–6

1 × 275 g (9½ oz) packet wonton
  wrappers
coriander (cilantro) leaves and sliced
  spring onion (scallion), to garnish

WONTON FILLING
2 coriander (cilantro) stalks,
  well washed
3 cm (1¼ in) piece of ginger, peeled
1 garlic clove, minced
2 spring onions (scallions),
  thinly sliced
1 teaspoon Asian chilli paste
  (more or less to taste)
100 g (3½ oz) medium/firm tofu
200 g (7 oz) fresh veggie mince
30 g (1 oz) dried shiitake
  mushrooms, soaked and finely
  chopped
20 g (¾ oz) dried black fungus
  (wood ears), soaked and finely
  chopped
1 tablespoon shaoxing rice wine
1 tablespoon soy sauce
1 teaspoon caster (superfine)
  or granulated sugar
white pepper
½ teaspoon salt
2 teaspoons cornflour (cornstarch)

CHILLI OIL SAUCE
125 ml (4 fl oz/½ cup) Sichuan chilli
  oil (page 164)
2 tablespoons black vinegar
1 small handful chopped coriander
  (cilantro) leaves
½ teaspoon caster (superfine)
  or granulated sugar

To make the wonton filling, place the coriander stalks, ginger, garlic, spring onion and chilli paste in a food processor and blitz to a rough paste. Add the remaining ingredients and pulse until well combined but not totally smooth.

Spoon 1 teaspoon of the filling mixture onto each wonton wrapper and fold into your desired dumpling shape. Use your finger to wet the edges with water and pinch to seal, then place on a lined tray.

Bring a large saucepan of water to the boil, then reduce to a gentle simmer. Working in batches, carefully drop the wontons into the water and cook for 2–3 minutes. Remove with a slotted spoon and place in a bowl.

Meanwhile, to make the sauce, combine all the ingredients in a small bowl.

Garnish the wontons with coriander and spring onion and serve with the chilli oil sauce.

There is never a bad time of the day to eat fried rice. I put breakfast in the recipe title to make it socially acceptable for you to knock this together and eat it first thing – you're welcome. As always, fried rice is better made with day-old rice.

Begin by making the egg mixture. Place all the ingredients in a high-powered blender and blend until smooth.

Heat the oil in a wok over a medium heat, then pour the egg mixture over the base. Allow to cook untouched for 15 seconds before lightly scrambling with a spatula, then cook untouched for another 15 seconds. Scramble again and cook for another 30 seconds, then scoop into a bowl. Set aside.

Wipe out the wok and increase the heat to high. Add the butter and melt, then add the spring onion and mushroom and stir-fry for 30 seconds. Add the chilli, garlic and sausage and stir-fry for 1 minute, or until the sausage and mushroom are slightly golden.

Throw in the greens and quickly toss for 30 seconds, or until wilted. Season well with salt and white pepper. Add the rice and break up any clumps, then pour in the Maggi seasoning and toss well to coat. Push the rice to one side of the wok and add the cooked egg mixture. Break it up into smaller pieces with the spatula, then toss it through the rice. Finish with a good scattering of coriander and serve.

SERVES 4–6

1 tablespoon vegetable oil
40 g (1½ oz) butter
2 spring onions (scallions), sliced
5 large button mushrooms, sliced
½–1 long red or bird's eye chilli, sliced
1 garlic clove, minced
2 sausages, sliced (use your favourite)
2 big handfuls of leafy baby greens, like spinach and kale
white pepper
555 g (1 lb 4 oz/3 cups) cooked jasmine, medium-grain or long-grain rice (straight from the fridge is best)
1½ tablespoons Maggi seasoning sauce or light soy sauce
1 handful chopped coriander (cilantro) leaves

EGG MIXTURE
150 g (5½ oz) silken or soft tofu
1 tablespoon cornflour (cornstarch)
2 tablespoons oat or soy milk
pinch of ground turmeric
½ teaspoon black salt

Korean mung bean pancakes

These pancakes are one of the easiest things you will ever make. At first, the recipe may sound complicated, or even a bit overly sophisticated, but nothing could be further from the truth. If you can knock together a plain pancake without setting the house on fire, you got this. Feel free to make the pancakes any size you like. The batter keeps well in the fridge for a few days, so only cook what you need when you need it.

Drain the mung beans and place in a blender or food processor with the cold water. Blend until smooth and creamy, then pour into a large bowl and add the remaining ingredients (except the mayo and oil). Season with black pepper, mix well, then leave to stand for 5 minutes.

Heat a splash of oil in a frying pan over a medium heat, add 2 tablespoons of the batter and smooth out to a thin pancake (about 5 mm/¼ in thick). Cook for 2 minutes, or until golden, then flip and cook the other side for another 2-3 minutes. Remove and cover to keep warm while you cook the remaining pancakes. Serve with mayo, extra kimchi and extra spring onion, if desired, or just as they are.

SERVES 4–6

200 g (7 oz/1 cup) dried whole
  mung beans, soaked for at least
  6 hours or overnight
250 ml (8½ fl oz/1 cup) cold water
150 g (5½ oz) rice flour
200 g (7 oz) kimchi, chopped,
  plus extra to serve (optional)
3 spring onions (scallions),
  thinly sliced, plus extra to serve
  (optional)
2 tablespoons grated ginger
2 garlic cloves, minced
100 g (3½ oz) soy bean sprouts
  or bean sprouts
1–2 teaspoons salt
vegetable oil, for pan-frying
Kewpie mayo, to serve (optional)

This beloved Smith & Daughters recipe has done its dash at the restaurant, so I am sharing it here so you can replicate it at home, to the resounding applause of your friends and family. My gift to you.

MAKES 8–12 PIECES

8–12 thick slices of bread
 (whatever kind you like,
 though stale is better)
butter, for pan-frying
115 g (4 oz/½ cup) caster
 (superfine) sugar mixed with
 2 teaspoons ground cinnamon

BATTER
500 ml (17 fl oz/2 cups) soy or
 oat milk
40 g (1½ oz/⅓ cup) cornflour
 (cornstarch)
1 teaspoon vanilla paste or extract
2 tablespoons caster (superfine)
 sugar
½ teaspoon ground cinnamon
pinch of black salt

To make the batter, mix all the ingredients in a bowl until well combined.

Dip one slice of bread at a time into the batter, ensuring that it is well coated.

Heat a non-stick frying pan over a medium heat and melt 20 g (¾ oz) of butter for each batch. Depending on the size of your pan, you can cook one or two pieces of toast at a time. Fry without moving for 2 minutes, then have a little peek and check the colour of the crust – you're looking for a beautiful golden brown. Cook until you have exactly that, then flip and repeat on the other side.

As soon as the toast is golden on both sides, transfer it to a serving dish and sprinkle liberally with cinnamon sugar. If you have some poached fruit handy, serve it on top.

Classically, these all-the-rage-right-now pancakes are made with whipped egg whites, which give them their airy texture and impressive height. This vegan version is fluffy and super impressive for when you want to amaze your friends, but please note that when I say a ring mould is essential to the success of this recipe, I mean it.

Combine all the wet ingredients in a jug and leave to stand for 5 minutes. The mixture will thicken slightly.

Sift all the dry ingredients into a medium mixing bowl with a pinch of salt and make a well in the middle. Pour the wet mixture into the dry and, using a spatula, gently fold the dry into the wet, mixing only until there are no visible dry spots. You need to keep the mixture light and airy for this to work.

Spray a heavy-based cast-iron frying pan with non-stick spray and warm over a low heat for a few minutes. For these pancakes to do the whole soufflé thing, they need the assistance of metal ring moulds. The higher the sides, the higher you can get your pancakes. Spray the inside of four high-sided ring moulds and place two in the pan (it's best to cook them in two batches as you need space to flip them). Fill with 2–3 tablespoons of the mixture, depending how high you'd like them.

Once the mix is in and level, place a lid on the pan and allow to cook for 5 minutes. Remove the lid and flip the pancake while still in the mould. Place the lid back on the pan and cook for another 2 minutes. To test whether they are cooked through, press on the top of a pancake – if there is slight resistance, you should be good to go. Repeat to make the remaining pancakes. Top with whatever you damn well please, but I love maple syrup.

MAKES 4 FAT-ARSE PANCAKES

non-stick cooking spray
maple syrup, to serve

WET
100 ml (3½ fl oz) milk
100 ml (3½ fl oz) soda water (club soda)
2 tablespoons apple-cider vinegar
2 tablespoons vegetable oil
1 teaspoon vanilla extract

DRY
200 g (7 oz/1⅓ cups) plain (all-purpose) flour
50 g (1¾ oz) icing (confectioners') sugar
2 teaspoons baking powder
½ teaspoon bicarbonate of soda (baking soda)

MINIMUM EFFORT, MAXIMUM RESULTS

LUNCH AND DINNER FOR BUSY PEOPLE

Let's face it: cooking is not always relaxing and therapeutic, and there are times when you just need to get the week's food situation sorted. I also fully appreciate that, while you want to eat well, cooking may not be the thing that lights you up. It's smart to plan ahead when you're choosing to eat vegan so you can avoid having to order the depressing vegan option from the office cafeteria or coming home to deal with the minefield that is food delivery. Here is a collection of quick, easy and affordable recipes that you can prep at the start of the week, taking you from lunch al desko to lazy mid-week dinner and beyond.

Is it mashed potato? Is it a sandwich spread? Nobody really knows! But if there's one thing we DO know it's that this Japanese potato salad is bloody delicious ... and who can hate a salad you can serve with an ice-cream scoop?

SERVES 4–6

3 large potatoes (approximately
  800 g/1 lb 12 oz), peeled and diced
1 × 5 cm (2 in) piece of dried kombu
½ small brown onion, finely
  chopped
1 small carrot, peeled, quartered
  lengthways, then thinly sliced
80 g (2¾ oz/½ cup) frozen peas
125 g (4½ oz/½ cup) Mayonnaise
  (page 167) or Kewpie mayo
2 tablespoons rice vinegar
1 teaspoon hot English mustard
white pepper
1 small Lebanese cucumber,
  thinly sliced
shredded nori, to serve (optional)

Place the diced potato in a colander and rinse under cold running water to remove excess starch. Transfer to a saucepan and cover with cold water, along with a big pinch of salt. Drop in the kombu and bring to the boil, then reduce the heat and simmer until the potato can be easily pierced with a knife.

Remove and discard the kombu, then drain the potato, leaving it to sit in the colander for a few minutes to dry out. Tip it back into the saucepan and mash until there are no large lumps, then transfer to a bowl and allow to cool to room temperature.

Meanwhile, fill a small saucepan with water and bring to the boil. Add a pinch of salt, then blanch the onion, carrot and peas for 1 minute. Drain and refresh under cold running water.

Stir the mayo, vinegar and mustard through the cooled potato mash until well combined and season with salt and white pepper. Add the onion, carrot, peas and cucumber and mix one last time. Best eaten cold, served with an ice-cream scoop. Finish with a sprinkling of shredded nori if you like.

It sounds a bit posh, but this salad is very easy to make. Beautiful for lunch, or make it for a fancy dinner party when you want to impress.

Heat a chargrill pan or barbecue grill plate until smoking hot. Drizzle the asparagus with olive oil and season with salt and pepper. Grill until char lines develop, then transfer to a bowl. Repeat with the radicchio, then add to the bowl along with the asparagus.

Place the peach halves on the grill and turn often until char marks appear on all sides. Peel off the skins if you like, then tear the peaches into bite-sized chunks or cut into quarters and add to the bowl.

To make the dressing, place all the ingredients in a jar, season with salt and pepper and shake well to combine.

Add the mint and basil leaves to the bowl and dress the salad with as much or as little dressing as you like. I prefer my salads heavily dressed. Any leftover dressing will keep in the fridge for up to a week.

SERVES 4–6

2 bunches asparagus (about 12 large
   spears), woody ends trimmed,
   halved
extra-virgin olive oil, for drizzling
½ radicchio, core removed,
   cut into 3 wedges
4 yellow or white peaches, halved,
   stones removed
1 handful mint leaves
1 handful basil leaves

DRESSING
125 ml (4 fl oz/½ cup)
   extra-virgin olive oil
juice of 1 large lemon
½ shallot, finely diced
1 teaspoon dijon mustard

Caesar salad has long been the king of salads, and for good reason. I could tell you the history of this dish, but that's what Wikipedia is for. Just eat it and be happy.

SERVES 4–6

extra-virgin olive oil
3 good handfuls of torn stale bread
2 baby cos (romaine) lettuces, outer
  leaves roughly chopped, small
  inner leaves kept whole
6 slices of bacon, sliced into strips
  and fried (you could also use
  smoked tofu)
finely grated or shaved parmesan,
  to serve

DRESSING
250 g (9 oz/1 cup) Mayonnaise
  (page 167)
2 tablespoons worcestershire sauce
1 garlic clove, minced
1 teaspoon dijon mustard
2 tablespoons lemon juice
½ teaspoon black salt
3 tablespoons finely grated parmesan

To make the dressing, whisk all the ingredients in a small bowl, season with pepper and set aside.

Heat a good splash of olive oil in a frying pan over a medium–high heat. Add the torn bread and fry until golden brown. Remove and drain on paper towel, then sprinkle with a little salt.

Place the cos lettuce, bacon and two-thirds of the croutons in a large mixing bowl. Pour over as much dressing as you like and mix well to coat the lettuce. Lay out on a serving plate, then finish with the parmesan and remaining croutons.

Any leftover dressing will keep in the fridge for up to a week.

Sometimes only a 50/50 carb to mayo ratio will do. This is the pasta salad that your imaginary hillbilly aunty would bring to a family barbecue and nobody would eat, but the second everyone left you would unashamedly dig in, standing alone in the dark in your kitchen.

SERVES 4–6

400 g (14 oz) dried elbow macaroni
1 small red onion, finely chopped
2 carrots, peeled and grated
2 celery stalks, finely diced,
   plus leaves from the celery heart,
   to garnish (see page 180 for what
   to do with the bitter outer leaves)
1 handful flat-leaf (Italian) parsley
   leaves, chopped

DRESSING
250 g (9 oz/1 cup) Mayonnaise
   (page 167)
2 tablespoons apple-cider vinegar
1 teaspoon caster (superfine) sugar
½ teaspoon celery seeds
1 tablespoon American mustard

Cook the macaroni in salted boiling water until al dente. Drain and refresh under cold running water. Drain again.

To make the dressing, whisk all the ingredients together.

Place the pasta and all the remaining salad ingredients in a large bowl. Pour over the dressing (I like to use all of it), season to taste with salt and pepper and mix well to combine. Refrigerate for 1 hour. Garnish with the celery leaves and serve.

Cabbage, radish and cucumber salad

The Schwarzenegger of salads! Vegan mayo travels well, so this is a great salad to take to potlucks and picnics or on the plane for properly delicious vegan sustenance.

Using either a mandoline or a food processor fitted with a thin slicing blade, finely shred the cabbage, then thinly slice the cucumbers and radishes. Place the cucumber in a sieve or colander and sprinkle with a big pinch of salt. Allow to stand for 15 minutes to remove any excess moisture, then pat dry with paper towel.

To make the dressing, place all the ingredients in a jar, season with salt and pepper and shake well to combine.

Combine the cabbage, cucumber, radish and herbs in a bowl, then pour over the dressing and mix together well.

SERVES 4–6

¼ green cabbage
  (approximately 500 g/1 lb 2 oz)
2 Lebanese (short) cucumbers
5 large radishes
1 large handful dill, roughly chopped
1 large handful flat-leaf (Italian)
  parsley leaves, roughly chopped

DRESSING
125 g (4½ oz/½ cup) sour cream
3 tablespoons Mayonnaise
  (page 167)
3 tablespoons apple-cider vinegar
2 tablespoons water
1 small shallot, finely diced

French onion soup

Not all onions are created equal! Some bring that special heat, some are more mellow and sweet. Some cook down to nothing, while others hold their shape. Here, each type of onion plays a part in the rich development of flavour that makes this the only French onion soup recipe you'll ever need. Of course, you can use whatever you have, but I promise you it's worth tracking all these babies down and giving it a proper go.

What you can do to make this recipe easier is to use a food processor with a slicing blade attachment to make the chopping process faster and less weepy.

Heat the oil and 150 g (5½ oz) of the butter in a heavy-based saucepan over a medium heat. Add the onions and shallots, then reduce the heat to low and cook, stirring occasionally, for about 20 minutes, or until softened. Season with the salt and pepper and continue to cook, stirring occasionally, for another 45 minutes, or until the onion mixture is a deep golden brown. If it starts to stick, add a tiny amount of water.

Pour in the wines and sherry and increase the heat to high. Cook until the wine has reduced by half, then add the thyme, bay leaves and stock. Bring to the boil, then reduce the heat to low and simmer for 30 minutes. Remove from the heat and whisk in the cornflour slurry and remaining 40 g (1½ oz) butter until melted and well combined. Adjust the seasoning to taste.

Heat a frying pan over a medium heat. Butter one side of each slice of bread, then make sandwiches with the cheese (saving a bit for later), ensuring the slices are buttered side out. Add to the pan and cook until golden on both sides (like you're making grilled cheese sandwiches). Remove and rub with the cut side of the garlic clove.

Place ramekins or oven-safe bowls on a baking tray and ladle in the soup. Top with the grilled cheese toasts.

Divide the remaining cheese among the bowls, covering the toast and some of the soup. Place the baking tray under a hot grill (broiler) and cook until the cheese has melted and the soup is bubbling.

SERVES 4–6

3 tablespoons extra-virgin olive oil

190 g (6½ oz) butter, plus extra for spreading

1 kg (2 lb 3 oz) brown onions, halved lengthways, peeled and thinly sliced

500 g (1 lb 2 oz) red onions, halved lengthways, peeled and thinly sliced

500 g (1 lb 2 oz) cipollini onions, halved lengthways, peeled and thinly sliced

500 g (1 lb 2 oz) shallots, halved lengthways, peeled and thinly sliced

2 teaspoons salt flakes

1 teaspoon pepper

250 ml (8½ fl oz/1 cup) white wine

250 ml (8½ fl oz/1 cup) Madeira or marsala wine

250 ml (8½ fl oz/1 cup) dry sherry

½ bunch thyme, tied

2 bay leaves

2.5 litres (85 fl oz/10 cups) beef stock

1 teaspoon cornflour (cornstarch) blended with 2 tablespoons water

1 pipe loaf or baguette, cut into 5 mm (¼ in) thick slices

200 g (7 oz) grated cheese

1 garlic clove, halved lengthways

Anyone who says they hate chicken and sweetcorn soup is a liar. Keep at least one container of this delightful soup in the freezer and bust it out when you need something healing and delicious in a snap.

Heat the oil in a large saucepan over a medium heat and cook the ginger, garlic and whites of the spring onion for 1–2 minutes, or until they begin to soften. Add the creamed corn and shaoxing wine and cook for 1 minute, then add the corn kernels, soy sauce and stock. Bring to the boil, then reduce the heat to low and simmer for 15 minutes. Stir in the sesame oil.

Place the egg drop ingredients and 125 ml (4 fl oz/½ cup) broth from the pan in a high-powered blender and blend until smooth.

Slowly pour the egg drop mix into the soup in a steady stream, stirring constantly. Cook for another 2 minutes, then season with salt and the white pepper. Ladle into bowls and garnish with the green part of the spring onions.

Pictured page 59

SERVES 4–6

3 tablespoons vegetable oil
6 cm (2½ in) piece of ginger, peeled and julienned
2 large garlic cloves, minced
3 spring onions (scallions), thinly sliced, white and green parts separated
1 × 400 g (14 oz) tin creamed corn
2 tablespoons shaoxing rice wine
300 g (10½ oz) fresh or frozen corn kernels
2 tablespoons light soy sauce
600 ml (20½ fl oz) chicken stock
1 teaspoon sesame oil
white pepper

EGG DROP MIX
100 g (3½ oz) silken tofu
3 tablespoons plain (all-purpose) flour

There are many uses for stale bread: ducks at the park, the Baked colcannon on page 87, or this recipe. Leftover bread can add body and substance to soups. You eat bread with soup anyway ... this recipe just cuts out the middle man.

SERVES 4–6

3 tablespoons extra-virgin olive oil, plus extra to serve
1 brown onion, finely chopped
3 garlic cloves, minced
1 teaspoon fennel seeds
1 teaspoon chilli flakes
1 kg (2 lb 3 oz) peeled tomatoes (fresh or tinned)
1 tablespoon tomato paste (concentrated purée)
1 litre (34 fl oz/4 cups) water
150 g (5½ oz) stale bread, crusts removed, cut into cubes
pinch of caster (superfine) or granulated sugar (optional)
1 handful basil leaves, torn
1 teaspoon balsamic vinegar
Carrot top pesto (page 173), to serve (optional)

Heat the oil in a large saucepan over a medium heat, add the onion and cook for a few minutes until soft and slightly golden. Toss in the garlic, fennel seeds and chilli flakes and cook for another minute. Add the tomatoes, season with salt and pepper and cook until the tomatoes are really soft and broken down, about 10 minutes.

Using a hand-held blender, purée the tomato mixture until very smooth, then add the tomato paste and water and stir to combine. Stir in the bread, then reduce the heat to low and simmer for 15–20 minutes, or until the bread has completely broken down.

Check the seasoning and add a little sugar if the tomatoes aren't quite sweet enough. Finish with the basil and vinegar (or a drizzle of pesto if you have some). Ladle into bowls, garnish with a big splash of extra olive oil and serve.

Pictured page 59

This is the ultimate 'I can't be f*cked' dinner. If you're under the weather or hungover and the situation shows no signs of improving, break out this recipe and it will cure what ails you.

SERVES 4–6

3 tablespoons extra-virgin olive oil

1 large brown onion, sliced

1 bulb fennel, cored and sliced, fronds reserved and chopped

3 large garlic cloves, minced

1 teaspoon chilli flakes

1 × 400 g (14 oz) tin chickpeas, drained and rinsed

1 bunch silverbeet (Swiss chard), stalks sliced, leaves shredded

250 g (9 oz) flat pasta (broken lasagne sheets work well)

1.5 litres (51 fl oz/6 cups) chicken or vegetable stock

finely grated zest and juice of 1 lemon

1 handful chopped flat-leaf (Italian) parsley leaves

1 handful grated parmesan, plus extra to serve

Heat the oil in large shallow saucepan over a medium heat, add the onion, fennel and a big pinch of salt and cook for a few minutes until they begin to soften and turn a light golden colour. Add the garlic and chilli flakes and cook for 1 minute. Add the chickpeas and silverbeet stalks, then reduce the heat to medium–low and cook for another 2 minutes. Toss through the silverbeet leaves and cook until they begin to wilt. Add the pasta and stock and bring to the boil. Season well, then reduce the heat to low and cook, covered, for 10 minutes.

Remove the lid and stir through the lemon zest and juice and half the parsley. Cook uncovered for another minute or two to slightly reduce the liquid. Add a good handful of parmesan and stir through until melted.

Add the fennel fronds and remaining parsley and check the seasoning. Ladle into bowls and serve garnished with plenty more parmesan.

Vegans and dahl, I get it. But if you have to have it on high rotation, throw all your other dahl recipes in the bin and use this one. A cheap, nutritionally dense dish that's perfect for vegans and non-vegans alike.

Place the onion, garlic, ginger, green chilli and coriander root in a blender and blitz to a paste.

Melt the butter in a large saucepan over a low heat, add the paste and cook for 5 minutes. Stir in the salt, turmeric, chilli powder, ground cumin and ground coriander.

Add the lentils and stir to coat, then pour in the water and season well with pepper. Add the beans, then partially cover and simmer for 20 minutes. Stir through the garam masala, spinach, then the yoghurt and cook for another 5 minutes. Add more water if it needs thinning down. Once it reaches the consistency you like, you're done!

SERVES 4–6

2 brown onions, roughly chopped
4 garlic cloves
6 cm (2½ in) piece of ginger, peeled
   and roughly chopped
2–3 green chillies, sliced
roots from 1 bunch coriander
   (cilantro), cleaned
80 g (2¾ oz) butter or ghee
1 teaspoon salt
1 teaspoon ground turmeric
1 teaspoon chilli powder
2 teaspoons ground cumin
2 teaspoons ground coriander
250 g (9 oz/1 cup) red lentils
1 litre (34 fl oz/4 cups) water,
   plus extra if needed
1 × 400 g (14 oz) tin beans of your
   choice (I like red kidney beans)
1 teaspoon garam masala
½ bunch English spinach, roughly
   chopped (use frozen or baby
   spinach if you like)
125 g (4½ oz/½ cup) plain yoghurt

You've all heard of it, but how many of you actually know what it is? It's time to change that because this filling, spice-spiked classic is a vegan's best pal.

SERVES 4–6

3 tablespoons vegetable or
  coconut oil
1 brown onion, finely chopped
3 garlic cloves, minced
½ bunch greens of choice (such as
  kale or Chinese broccoli/gai lan),
  chopped
2 teaspoons Caribbean spice mix
¼ teaspoon ground allspice
400 g (14 oz/2 cups) long-grain
  or jasmine rice
3 tablespoons of your favourite
  hot sauce
1 × 400 g (14 oz) tin kidney or
  black beans, drained and rinsed
1 × 400 ml (13½ fl oz) tin
  coconut milk
2 thyme sprigs
1 bay leaf
625 ml (21 fl oz/2½ cups) water
1 chicken stock cube (optional)
juice of 1 lime or ½ lemon
1 handful chopped coriander
  (cilantro) leaves (optional)

Heat the oil in a wide shallow saucepan over a medium heat. Add the onion and a pinch of salt and cook for a few minutes until softened. Add the garlic and cook for another minute, then toss in the chopped greens and cook until wilted. Add the spice mix and allspice and stir well to combine.

Pour the rice over the vegetables and cook, stirring, until the grains are coated in the spiced oil. Stir in the hot sauce, then add the beans, coconut milk, thyme, bay leaf, water and stock cube (if using). Bring to the boil, then reduce the heat to low and simmer, covered, for 20 minutes, or until the liquid has been absorbed and the rice is cooked.

Fluff up the rice mixture with a fork and squeeze over the lime. Garnish with coriander, if you like, and serve.

Minimum effort, maximum results

Glossy, silky-soft rice noodles, turbo savoury flavours, and all the magic of that breath of the wok – this is a Malaysian classic worth getting to know.

To make the egg mix, place all the ingredients in a high-powered blender and blend until smooth. Set aside.

For the sauce, mix together all the ingredients in a small bowl.

Heat a wok over a high heat – you want it to be smoking hot when you start cooking.

Add the oil, throw in the mushrooms and garlic shoots and quickly stir-fry for 30 seconds. Add the minced garlic and chilli paste and toss to combine, then add the cabbage and spring onion and cook, tossing, until the cabbage begins to wilt.

Scatter over the noodles and toss, then add the bean sprouts. Toss again to combine and cook for 30 seconds.

Push the noodle mixture to one side of the wok, then, working in two batches, pour the egg mix into the base of the wok and scramble with a spatula. Mix the first batch into the noodles, then repeat with the second batch. Once all the egg mix is cooked, toss with the noodles to combine.

Pour the sauce mixture over the noodles and toss through. Cook for a final 30 seconds, then serve.

SERVES 4–6

3 tablespoons vegetable oil
100 g (3½ oz) mushrooms
  (whatever is your favourite)
5 garlic shoots, cut into 3 cm
  (1¼ in) lengths
2 garlic cloves, minced
2 tablespoons Asian chilli paste
75 g (2¾ oz/1 cup) shredded
  Chinese cabbage (wombok)
3 spring onions (scallions), cut into
  5 cm (2 in) lengths
500 g (1 lb 2 oz) wide rice noodles,
  prepared according to the packet
  instructions
100 g (3½ oz) bean sprouts

EGG MIX
150 g (5½ oz) silken or soft tofu
1 tablespoon cornflour (cornstarch)
1 tablespoon oat or soy milk
pinch of ground turmeric
pinch of black salt

SAUCE
3 tablespoons dark soy sauce
2 tablespoons Maggi seasoning
  sauce or light soy sauce
2 tablespoons kecap manis
1 tablespoon oyster sauce
1 tablespoon fish sauce
2 teaspoons caster (superfine) sugar

A one-pot wonder. I came up with this recipe when I arrived home extremely jetlagged after a long few weeks of travel and needed to lie on the couch and just shovel something delicious into my face.

Orzo bolognese

SERVES 4–6

3 tablespoons extra-virgin olive oil
2 celery stalks, finely diced
1 brown onion, finely chopped
1 small carrot, peeled and
  finely diced
½ bulb fennel, finely diced
3 garlic cloves, minced
1 tablespoon capers in brine,
  roughly chopped
1 teaspoon chilli flakes (optional)
400 g (14 oz) veggie mince or
  soaked textured vegetable protein
2 tablespoons tomato paste
  (concentrated purée)
250 ml (8½ fl oz/1 cup) milk
250 ml (8½ fl oz/1 cup) red wine
700 ml (23½ fl oz) passata
  (puréed tomatoes)
375 ml (12½ fl oz/1½ cups)
  beef stock
1 bay leaf
250 g (9 oz) orzo
about 250 ml (8½ fl oz/1 cup) water
1 handful basil leaves, torn
1 handful flat-leaf (Italian) parsley
  leaves, roughly chopped
grated or shaved parmesan, to serve

Heat the oil in a large shallow saucepan over a medium heat, add the celery, onion, carrot, fennel and a big pinch of salt and cook for 3 minutes, or until the vegetables begin to soften and turn slightly golden. Add the garlic, capers and chilli flakes (if using) and cook for another minute.

Throw in the veggie mince or textured vegetable protein. If using mince, break it up into small pieces with your wooden spoon. Cook for 1 minute, making sure that everything is well combined, then stir in the tomato paste.

Pour in the milk and simmer until almost completely absorbed, then follow with the wine and cook until it has reduced by half. Add the passata and stock and chuck in your bay leaf. Season well with salt and pepper. Reduce the heat to medium–low and simmer for 30 minutes, stirring often.

Add the orzo and some or all of the water, depending on how dry your sauce is – you want it to look a little wetter than a regular bolognese. Cook for a further 15 minutes, or until the orzo is cooked through.

Stir through the basil and parsley, then spoon into bowls and cover with parmesan.

Australia's obsession with American culture has led us to believe that we should all be eating meatloaf. Perfect for mid-week meals and lunchboxes alike, this is an Australian take on an American pop culture classic. It makes an excellent addition to snack plates and sandwiches, or just enjoy it on its own, straight out of the fridge.

SERVES 4–6

non-stick cooking spray

WET INGREDIENTS
250 ml (8½ fl oz/1 cup) vegetable oil
1 small brown onion, grated
1 carrot, peeled and grated
1 large zucchini (courgette), grated
2 garlic cloves, minced
1 teaspoon chopped rosemary
1 teaspoon chopped thyme
finely grated zest of ½ lemon
100 g (3½ oz) medium/firm tofu, blended until smooth
1 tablespoon tomato paste (concentrated purée)
1 peeled small raw beetroot (beet) (approximately 120 g/4½ oz), puréed with 80 ml (2½ fl oz/ ⅓ cup) water
250 ml (8½ fl oz/1 cup) beef stock

DRY INGREDIENTS
150 g (5½ oz/1 cup) Vital Wheat gluten flour
80 g (2¾ oz/½ cup) potato flour
3 tablespoons besan (chickpea flour)

GLAZE
3 tablespoons tomato sauce (ketchup)
1 tablespoon dijon mustard
1 teaspoon maple syrup
½ teaspoon smoked paprika

Preheat the oven to 170°C (340°F) and generously spray a large loaf (bar) tin with non-stick cooking spray.

Start with the wet ingredients. Heat 80 ml (2½ fl oz/⅓ cup) of the oil in a frying pan over a medium heat, add the onion, carrot and zucchini and a big pinch of salt and cook for a few minutes until softened. Add the garlic and cook for another minute. Tip the cooked vegetables into a bowl and, when cool enough to handle, squeeze out as much liquid as possible and discard.

Meanwhile, mix together the dry ingredients in a large bowl.

Combine the cooked vegetables and remaining wet ingredients in a jug. Pour the wet mixture into the dry and mix well. Spoon the mixture into the prepared tin and press well to ensure there are no air pockets. Cover with foil and bake for 30 minutes, then remove from the oven.

To make the glaze, combine all the ingredients in a small bowl.

Remove the foil from the meatloaf and brush the glaze over the top. Return to the oven and bake, uncovered, for another 15 minutes, or until the meatloaf feels firm to the touch. Allow to cool in the tin for 10 minutes, then run a knife along the edges and turn it out onto a small board or plate glaze-side up (hands are okay too if it's not too hot). Cut into thick slices and serve at whatever temperature you want – it's great in a sandwich. It will keep well wrapped in the fridge for 4 days.

DINNER IS IN THE DETAILS

... OR IS IT?

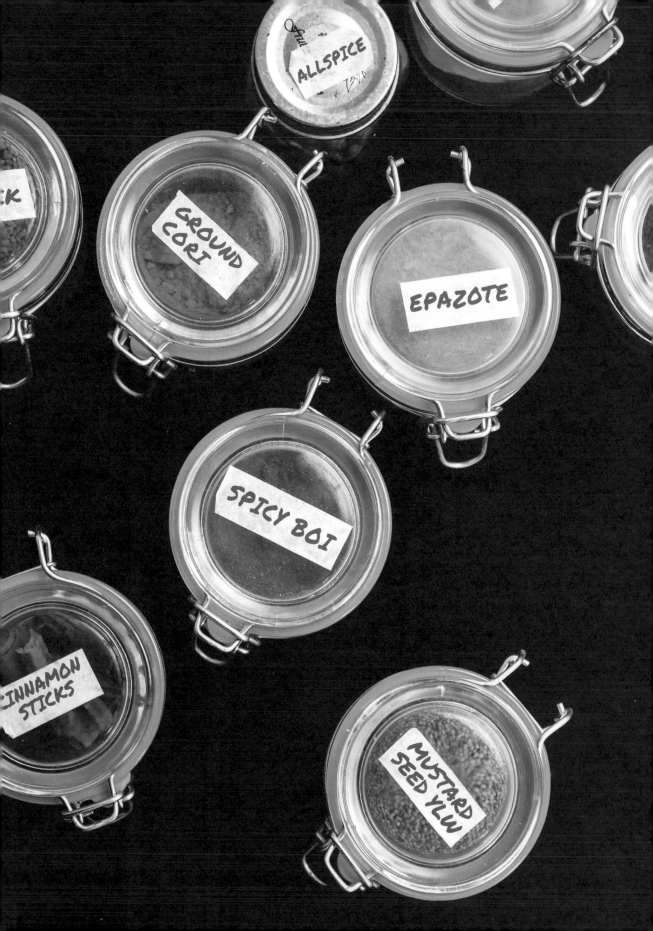

I am notorious for making vegan food with a heap of elements because I believe that layering flavours and textures is the best way to give it a multi-dimensional, goddamn delicious quality that rivals non-vegan dishes. That said, the intention of this book is to strip some of that back to a simpler format while still delivering the same quality of flavour. What sets these dishes apart from the everyday meals in the previous chapter is that they may have one or two more steps (and I have also included some sides that everyone should have in their repertoire). But I can guarantee you that each and every one of these recipes gives the big middle finger to those who think vegan food can't be awesome. Bust these recipes out when you need to impress your friends, your parents, or even yourself!

French fries and spring rolls: we love them for the same reason – they're crunchy, golden, salty and delicious. From little kids to big, these spring rolls are a crowd pleaser, perfect for entertaining, guilty-pleasure snacking or epic hangovers.

Set a wok over a high heat until smoking hot, then add the oil and swirl to coat.

Add the ginger, garlic, spring onion and pickled vegetables and cook for 1 minute, then add the carrot and cabbage and stir-fry until the cabbage has wilted. Toss in the fungus, bamboo shoots and bean sprouts and stir-fry for another minute.

Quickly stir through the Maggi seasoning, sugar and coriander and season with salt and white pepper. Toss to combine, then transfer to a bowl to cool. Wipe out the wok as you'll be using it again to deep-fry the rolls.

Place a spring roll wrapper on a board with one corner pointing towards you (cover the remaining wrappers with a damp tea towel/dish towel to stop them drying out). Brush the edges with the cornflour slurry, then spoon 1 tablespoon of the vegetable mixture onto the corner of the wrapper. Fold the corner over the filling, then roll up from corner to corner, folding in the edges to enclose the filling. Repeat with the remaining wrappers and filling.

Pour oil into the wok until one-third full and heat over a high heat until a small piece of bread dropped into the oil sizzles. Add the spring rolls in batches (so you don't overcrowd the pan) and cook for 3–4 minutes, or until golden. Remove with a slotted spoon and drain on a wire rack set over a baking tray. Serve hot with your choice of dipping sauce, fresh herbs and lettuce.

MAKES ABOUT 40

2 tablespoons vegetable oil, plus extra for deep-frying

3 cm (1¼ in) piece of ginger, peeled and grated

2 garlic cloves, minced

2 spring onions (scallions), thinly sliced

100 g (3½ oz) Sichuan pickled vegetables or mustard greens

1 carrot, peeled and shredded

225 g (8 oz/3 cups) shredded Chinese cabbage (wombok)

10 g (¼ oz/⅓ cup) dried black fungus (wood ears), soaked and shredded

75 g (2¾ oz) bamboo shoots, finely chopped

90 g (3 oz/1 cup) bean sprouts

2 tablespoons Maggi seasoning sauce or light soy sauce

½ teaspoon caster (superfine) sugar

1 small handful coriander (cilantro) leaves, chopped

white pepper

1 × 275 g (9½ oz) packet spring roll wrappers

2 teaspoons cornflour (cornstarch) blended with 2 tablespoons cold water

soy sauce or sweet chilli sauce, to serve

Kofta

As a rule in this book, I am steering clear of mock meat because it drives up the cost of a dish, and that's the opposite of my goal here. As with real meat (if you eat it), I suggest you consider mock meat a luxury rather than a staple.

SERVES 4–6

extra-virgin olive oil, for brushing
  and drizzling
Tzatziki and Flatbreads (pages 159
  and 151), to serve

KOFTA

500 g (1 lb 2 oz) fresh veggie mince
  (this is essential, do not substitute)
½ red onion, grated
3 garlic cloves, minced
40 g (1½ oz/½ cup) fresh
  breadcrumbs
1 tablespoon ground coriander
2 teaspoons ground cumin
1 teaspoon ground cinnamon
½ teaspoon ground allspice
½ teaspoon dried mint
1–2 tablespoons harissa paste
  (depending on how spicy
  you like it)
1 tablespoon finely chopped
  preserved lemon or finely grated
  zest of 1 lemon
1–2 teaspoons salt
1 small handful chopped coriander
  (cilantro) leaves
1 small handful chopped flat-leaf
  (Italian) parsley leaves
100 g (3½ oz) medium/firm tofu,
  crumbled

To make the kofta, place all the ingredients except the tofu in a bowl and mix well with your hands. Season with black pepper, then add the crumbled tofu and gently mix until just combined.

Either form the kofta around skewers or simply make oval patties. Make them whatever size you like.

Heat a chargrill pan or barbecue grill plate over a medium–high heat and brush with oil. Once the pan is hot, add the koftas and cook for 3–4 minutes, or until a golden charred crust has developed, then turn and repeat on the other side. Serve with tzatziki and flatbreads, with a final drizzle of oil.

Creamed silverbeet with preserved lemon

Not all vegan food is healthy – and thank god for that – but this recipe is one way to get people to eat an entire bunch of silverbeet in one go.

Melt the butter in a large shallow saucepan over a medium heat, add the onion and cook for a few minutes until slightly golden. Add the garlic, chilli flakes and lemon and cook for another minute.

Add the silverbeet, then pour over enough stock to half-cover it. Reduce the heat to low and cook, covered, for 30 minutes, stirring occasionally. Remove the lid, then increase the heat to medium and simmer until the liquid has reduced by half. Add the cream cheese and stir until melted through. Season to taste and serve.

SERVES 4–6

20 g (¾ oz) butter
½ brown onion, thinly sliced
2 garlic cloves, minced
½ teaspoon chilli flakes
1 tablespoon finely chopped preserved lemon or finely grated zest of 1 lemon
1 bunch silverbeet (Swiss chard), trimmed, stalks and leaves thinly sliced
about 500 ml (17 fl oz/2 cups) vegetable stock
3 tablespoons cream cheese

Ever since eating this dish during my first trip to Barcelona, I crave it regularly. Creamy, acidic, peppery ... it's perfect for hot days when you want something nourishing but refreshing.

SERVES 4–6

800 g (1 lb 12 oz) cooked butter beans or other large white beans (tinned is fine)

3 celery stalks, finely diced, plus leaves from the celery heart

½ red capsicum (bell pepper), seeded and finely diced

1 tomato, seeded and diced

1 handful chopped flat-leaf (Italian) parsley leaves

80 ml (2½ fl oz/⅓ cup) extra-virgin olive oil

2 tablespoons sherry vinegar

Place everything in a large mixing bowl, season with salt and pepper and stir well. Allow the salad to sit for at least an hour before eating so that all the flavours have time to mingle.

You have a lot of countries in Europe claiming this recipe as theirs. Is it Greek, Italian, Turkish? Who cares? It's delicious!

SERVES 4–6

80 ml (2½ fl oz/⅓ cup) extra-virgin
  olive oil, plus extra to serve
1 brown onion, sliced
4 spring onions (scallions), sliced
4 garlic cloves, thinly sliced
1 kg (2 lb 3 oz) broad beans in
  the shell, podded (approximately
  350 g/12½ oz podded weight)
400 g (14 oz) prepared artichokes
1 teaspoon dried oregano
500 ml (17 fl oz/2 cups) chicken
  or vegetable stock
125 ml (4 fl oz/½ cup) lemon juice
1 bay leaf
finely grated zest of 1 lemon
chopped dill and mint leaves,
  to garnish

Heat the oil in a heavy-based wide shallow saucepan with a lid over a medium heat. Add the onion, spring onion and a pinch of salt and cook for a few minutes until slightly golden. Add the garlic and cook for another minute, then add the broad beans, artichokes and oregano and stir to coat. Pour over the stock and 3 tablespoons lemon juice, then throw in the bay leaf and season well with salt and pepper. Cover with a lid, then reduce the heat to low and simmer for 30 minutes, or until the beans and artichokes are soft.

Remove the lid and increase the heat to medium. Stir through the lemon zest and remaining lemon juice, then simmer until the liquid has reduced by one-third. Finish with plenty of dill and mint. Check the seasoning and add more if needed, then drizzle with a heap of extra oil and serve.

NOTE
You can use frozen broad beans and artichokes if you like. Look for them in Middle Eastern or Indian grocers.

Braised broad beans, artichokes and mint

Golden, crisp, fluffy, perfect.

Preheat the oven to 200°C (400°F).

Pour the hot water into a large saucepan and add the bicarbonate of soda, bay leaf and salt. Drop in the potato chunks and bring to the boil over a medium–high heat, then cook for 10 minutes, or until a knife can pierce a piece of potato but won't quite go all the way through.

Drain the potatoes and tip back into the pan. Drizzle generously with oil, season with salt and pepper and gently toss to coat. Spread out the potatoes in a single layer on a baking tray and roast untouched for 20 minutes. Remove from the oven and give the potatoes a toss, then roast for a further 30 minutes, or until golden and crispy, turning the potatoes every 10 minutes.

Just before you are ready to serve, heat 2 tablespoons oil in a small frying pan over a medium heat. Add the garlic and rosemary and cook for 1 minute, or until the garlic is slightly golden. Pour this mixture over the roast potatoes and toss to coat. Finish with a good pinch of salt and serve.

SERVES 4–6

2.5 litres (85 fl oz/10 cups) hot water

½ teaspoon bicarbonate of soda (baking soda)

1 bay leaf

3 teaspoons salt

1 kg (2 lb 3 oz) potatoes (yukon gold, desiree or kipflers are all good), peeled and halved if small, quartered if large

2 tablespoons extra-virgin olive oil, plus extra for drizzling

1 garlic clove, minced

1 rosemary sprig, leaves stripped and chopped

Tip: never trust a person who doesn't like mashed potato. Second tip: never trust a person who doesn't like mashed potato whipped with kale. You might have a spread of the most luxurious dishes in the world on the table, but you can bet your last dollar that this dish will be the first to disappear. With the simple addition of crunchy breadcrumbs and parmesan, you have a showstopper worthy of any VIP dinner guest.

SERVES 4–6

1 kg (2 lb 3 oz) potatoes (Dutch creams or desiree work well), peeled and diced
1 bay leaf
1 large bunch kale, stalks removed, leaves roughly chopped
375 ml (12½ fl oz/1½ cups) oat milk
3 spring onions (scallions), finely chopped
100 g (3½ oz) butter
white pepper
150 g (5½ oz) fresh breadcrumbs
2 tablespoons grated parmesan
extra-virgin olive oil, for drizzling

Preheat the oven to 180°C (350°F).

Place the potatoes in a medium saucepan, add the bay leaf and a big pinch of salt, and cover with cold water. Bring to the boil over a high heat, then reduce the heat to medium and simmer until a knife can easily pass through a piece of potato. Drain, discarding the bay leaf, then return the potatoes to the pan and put back over a low heat for 1 minute to steam off any excess moisture. Remove from the heat and mash the hot potatoes using your favourite method.

While the potatoes are cooking, bring a large saucepan of heavily salted water to the boil, drop in the kale and simmer for 5 minutes. Drain and refresh under cold running water, then squeeze out as much water as possible and finely chop. Set aside.

Rinse out the pan you cooked the kale in and pour in the milk. Add the spring onion and bring to the boil. Once boiling, turn off the heat and stir in the chopped kale. Add the mashed potato, drop in the butter and season with plenty of salt and white pepper. Whip the mixture with a wooden spoon until smooth and fluffy.

It's fine to eat as is, but I like to turn it up a little.

Scoop the colcannon into a baking dish. Mix together the breadcrumbs and parmesan, then sprinkle evenly over the surface. Drizzle with oil and bake for 20 minutes, or until golden. Season with salt and serve.

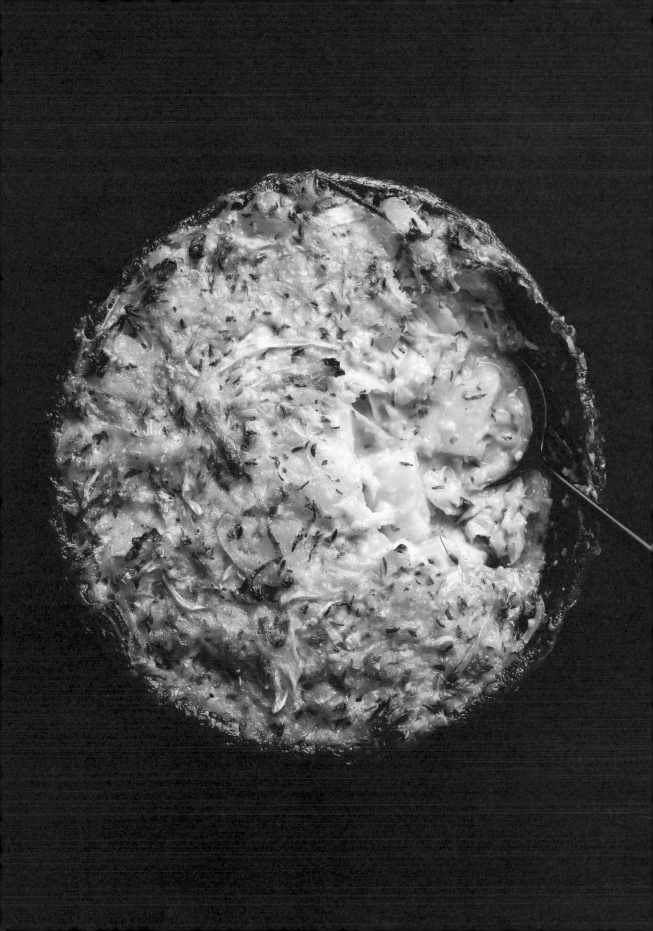

Sometimes, beige is the most delicious colour of all. This makes a fantastic side to roasts and more substantial dishes.

SERVES 4–6

3 large potatoes (approximately
  700 g/1 lb 9 oz), peeled and
  cut into 2 cm (¾ in) cubes
1 bay leaf
2 tablespoons extra-virgin olive oil
1 brown onion, thinly sliced
3 garlic cloves, minced
1½ teaspoons caraway seeds
½ savoy cabbage (approximately
  500 g/1 lb 2 oz), finely shredded
625 ml (21 fl oz/2½ cups) oat milk
185 g (6½ oz) shredded cheese
40 g (1½ oz) grated parmesan
  (optional)
3 tablespoons chopped tarragon
white pepper
40 g (1½ oz) butter

Preheat the oven to 200°C (400°F).

Place the potato cubes in a large saucepan, add the bay leaf and a huge pinch of salt, and cover with cold water. Bring to the boil over a high heat, then reduce the heat to medium and simmer for about 5 minutes, or until the potatoes have just begun to soften (you still want them to be a little firm). Drain the potatoes, discarding the bay leaf.

Heat the oil in a large frying pan over a medium heat, add the onion and cook for 3 minutes, or until soft and slightly golden. Add the garlic and caraway seeds and cook for another minute. Toss through the cabbage, then cook for a few minutes until softened. Scoop the cabbage mixture into a large mixing bowl, add the potatoes, milk, cheeses and tarragon and gently stir to combine. Season with salt and white pepper.

Pour the mixture into a medium baking dish and dot with the butter. Bake for 35–45 minutes, or until golden and bubbling.

Tom yum fried rice

Vegan tom yum paste is your secret weapon in the war on blandness. Keep it in your fridge and add it to almost anything (noodles, broth, a scramble) – you will have a tasty hero on your table in no time at all.

Set a wok over a high heat for a few minutes – you want this sucker to be HOT before you start cooking. Add the oil and swirl it around, then drop in the beans, mushrooms, broccoli stalks, pineapple, corn and onion and stir-fry for 1 minute, or until they begin to colour slightly. Add the tom yum paste and stir to coat the vegetables and pineapple, then throw in the cold rice. Quickly toss to mix everything together, then add the remaining ingredients and give it one final toss before serving.

NOTE

Cold leftover rice is best here, but if you don't have any, cook the rice and let it cool completely on a tray.

SERVES 4

3 tablespoons vegetable oil

100 g (3½ oz) snake (yard-long) beans or green beans, cut into 3 cm (1¼ in) lengths

80 g (2¾ oz) baby king brown mushrooms (or any mushrooms you like), halved

70 g (2½ oz) Chinese broccoli (gai lan), stalks chopped, leaves shredded

125 g (4½ oz) pineapple, peeled and chopped

75 g (2¾ oz/½ cup) frozen corn kernels

½ small brown onion, sliced

2 tablespoons tom yum paste

555 g (1 lb 4 oz/3 cups) cooked jasmine rice (see Note)

8 cherry tomatoes, halved

1 tablespoon fish sauce

1 tablespoon Maggi seasoning sauce or light soy sauce

chilli paste, chilli oil or chopped chilli, to taste (optional)

1 handful each of chopped coriander (cilantro) and Thai basil leaves

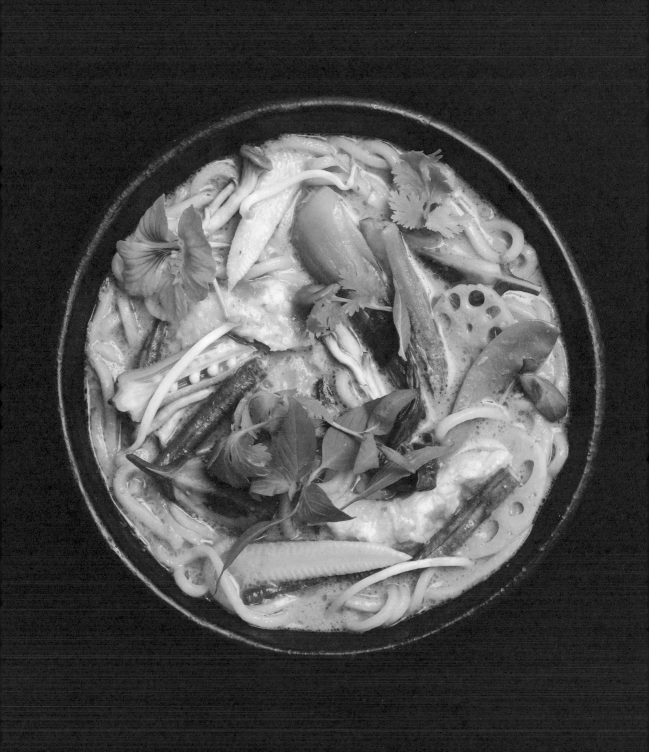

Laksa has basically become a national dish in Australia. Sure, you could go out for it, but this is one of those meals that is soooo satisfying to learn to make yourself. As you will see, some of the quantities are deliberately vague. Just use whatever veg are kicking around in your fridge and allow 50–75 grams of noodles (dry weight) per person. Dried rice vermicelli or fresh hokkien or rice noodles are all good.

SERVES 4–6

2 tablespoons vegetable oil
1 tablespoon curry powder
3 tablespoons fish sauce
50 g (1¾ oz) palm sugar (jaggery) or brown sugar
1 teaspoon salt
2 tablespoons Maggi seasoning sauce or light soy sauce
600 ml (20½ fl oz) coconut milk
600 ml (20½ fl oz) chicken or vegetable stock
6 kaffir lime leaves
veg of choice (zucchini/courgette, carrot, baby corn, potato, snow peas/mangetout, bok choy)
lime juice, to taste (optional)
handful each of coriander (cilantro) and Thai basil leaves
noodles, cooked according to the packet instructions

CURRY PASTE
½ teaspoon fennel seeds
1½ tablespoons coriander seeds
½ teaspoon cumin seeds
2 green cardamom pods, seeds only
8 dried red chillies, soaked (seeds removed for less heat)
1 lemongrass stem, white part only
3 cm (1¼ in) piece of galangal, grated
3 cm (1¼ in) piece of turmeric, grated
150 g (5½ oz) shallots
8–10 garlic cloves, peeled
4 cm (1½ in) piece of ginger, peeled
roots from ½ bunch coriander (cilantro), cleaned
1 tablespoon belacan paste (optional)

To make the curry paste, toast the fennel, coriander, cumin and cardamom seeds in a dry frying pan until aromatic. Remove and cool, then grind to a fine powder. Place the remaining ingredients in a high-powered blender and blend to a fairly smooth paste (add a tiny splash of water if needed). Add the spice powder and blitz again to combine.

Heat the oil in a wok over a medium–low heat, add 6 tablespoons of the paste (freeze the rest for another day) and cook for a few minutes until it no longer smells raw. Add the curry powder, fish sauce, sugar, salt and Maggi seasoning and stir until the sugar has melted. Cook for a few minutes, then add the coconut milk, stock, kaffir lime leaves and vegetables of choice and simmer gently until the veggies are just cooked.

Taste and add a squeeze of lime if needed and finish with the coriander and Thai basil. Serve in bowls over the noodles. Nasturtium flowers make for nice photos, but are not essential.

A southern Indian dish with a heap of sour tamarind, balanced out with sweet, rich coconut. People might shy away from this recipe because it may seem like she's a spicy gal, but don't let that stop you. When you remove the chilli seeds, it's a fantastic staple to add to a curry feast. She has punch, she has bite, she will win you over.

To make the masala paste, heat a large frying pan over a medium heat, add all the dry ingredients and dry-toast until fragrant. Add to a high-powered blender along with the remaining ingredients and blitz to a fairly smooth paste. Set aside.

Wipe out the pan, then add the oil and warm over a medium heat. Add the chillies, sprinkle with a little salt and cook until they are blistered on both sides, then remove with tongs and set aside.

Reheat the oil in the pan, then scatter in the curry leaves, turmeric and mustard and fenugreek seeds (if using). Watch out as this will spit a little. Cook for 15 seconds, then pour in the masala paste and cook until it begins to darken and dry out a little, about 4 minutes. Stir in the sugar, tamarind and water.

If you prefer, remove the skins from the chillies, otherwise just leave them. Drop the chillies into the pan and stir well to coat. Reduce the heat to low and cook, stirring often, for 15 minutes. Check the seasoning and you're done! Serve with rice if you like, or as a side.

SERVES 4–6

3 tablespoons vegetable oil
about 550 g (1 lb 3 oz) long green chillies, split down the middle with the stalk intact, seeds removed
2 sprigs curry leaves, leaves picked
1 teaspoon ground turmeric
1 teaspoon black mustard seeds
½ teaspoon fenugreek seeds (optional)
2 teaspoons brown sugar
3 tablespoons tamarind pulp
125 ml (4 fl oz/½ cup) water

MASALA PASTE
2 tablespoons sesame seeds
1 teaspoon poppy seeds
1 tablespoon chilli flakes (optional)
1 tablespoon coriander seeds
3 tablespoons raw peanuts
50 g (1¾ oz) unsweetened fresh or thawed frozen coconut
6 cm (2½ in) piece of ginger, peeled and roughly chopped
1 brown onion, chopped
4 garlic cloves, smashed and peeled
3 tablespoons water

Pea and ham soup is a winter staple in many Western households. Imagine amping it up with a host of vibrant, warming Indian spices, and you have the idea here ... maybe it's a dish that would have happened if India had occupied England instead of the other way around.

SERVES 4–6

6 cm (2½ in) piece of ginger, peeled
  and roughly chopped
4 garlic cloves
1 small red onion, roughly chopped
5 small green chillies
2 tablespoons coconut oil
1 teaspoon fennel seeds
4 whole cloves
1 teaspoon ground coriander
1 teaspoon chilli powder (optional)
½ teaspoon garam masala
½ teaspoon ground turmeric
2 tomatoes, diced
220 g (8 oz/1 cup) dried split green
  peas, soaked for 1 hour
1 litre (34 fl oz/4 cups) cold water,
  plus extra if needed
1 handful chopped coriander
  (cilantro) leaves

Place the ginger, garlic, onion and chillies in a blender and blitz to a fine paste.

Heat a heavy-based saucepan over a medium heat and add the coconut oil. Drop in the fennel seeds and cloves and fry for 15 seconds, then stir in the chilli paste.

Add the ground spices and fry for another minute – the mixture should look a little dry. Add the tomato and cook for a few minutes, or until it breaks down. Drain the split peas, then add to the pan and stir well to coat.

Pour in the water and bring to the boil, then reduce the heat to low and simmer for 30–40 minutes until the peas are soft. Add more water if it gets too dry. Season with plenty of salt and pepper, stir through the coriander and serve.

People think gnocchi are difficult to make, but they're not. It isn't about measurements, it's about feeling when the texture is right, which just comes with a little practice. Once you master it, you'll never forget.

SERVES 4–6

1.2 kg (2 lb 10 oz) potatoes (Dutch creams or russet reds work well)

about 110 g (4 oz/¾ cup) plain (all-purpose) flour (you may not use it all)

Preheat the oven to 200°C (400°F).

Place the potatoes, whole and unpeeled, on a baking tray and roast for 50–60 minutes, or until a knife can be easily inserted into the centre. Remove and cut in half to allow the steam to escape.

As soon as they are cool enough to handle, peel off the skins with your fingers and pass the potatoes through a ricer or mouli. If you don't have either of these, push them through a fine-mesh sieve or a colander with small holes. You don't want to be mashing them with a potato masher as this will overwork the potatoes and leave you with a very gummy gnocchi, which you absolutely don't want.

Dump the potato onto a floured bench and slowly start adding the flour, 3 tablespoons at a time. It's best to use something other than your hands at this stage. I use either a paint scraper or a cleaver and chop in the flour by dragging the mix onto itself from the outside to the middle, making sure the flour is evenly distributed. Continue until the dough is no longer sticky. The thing is, the more flour you add, the heavier and tougher the gnocchi will be, so only add what you need.

Once the dough is no longer sticky, bring it together with your hands and gently knead by pressing down onto it. This is different from bread dough, where you want to stretch it; with gnocchi we're just pressing, not stretching. If you need to add a little more flour at this point to keep it from sticking, go ahead, but keep it minimal. Once it feels like a nice soft playdough, shape it into a log and cut into five even pieces.

Working with one piece at a time, roll it with the palms of your hands to form a long snake. Roll it as thick as you like, depending on what size you'd like your gnocchi to be.

Once you have your snake, using a paint scraper or sharp knife, quickly cut the gnocchi into bite-sized pieces and place on a floured tray. Continue with the rest of the dough.

When all your dough has been turned into beautiful little pillows, place them, uncovered, in the fridge while you bring a large saucepan of heavily salted water to the boil.

Cook the gnocchi in batches so you don't overcrowd the pan. Drop them into the boiling water and keep watch. As soon as they float to the surface, give them another 30 seconds, then scoop them out of the water and place in a bowl. Once all the gnocchi are cooked, simply heat your sauce of choice in a frying pan, add the gnocchi and toss to coat!

Dan dan noodles

I want to introduce you to your new favourite dish. If you have been vegan for a long time, there is a chance you've never eaten a dish like this, and you absolutely should. It's creamy, punchy, spicy – everything you want in a bowl of noodles.

To make the sauce, whisk together all the ingredients in a medium bowl. Set aside while you prepare the rest of the recipe.

For the mince mixture, heat the oil in a wok over a medium–high heat and stir-fry the ginger, whites of the spring onion and pickled vegetables for 1 minute. Add the garlic and cook for a further 30 seconds. Add the mince or textured vegetable protein and stir well to combine, breaking it up into small bits if using veggie mince, then stir through the bean paste, shaoxing wine and dark soy sauce. Stir-fry for another minute, then remove from the heat and set aside.

Cook the noodles according to the packet instructions, then drain and place in a large bowl. Add some or all of the sauce, depending on how heavily dressed you like your noodles (I use it all!), and mix well to coat.

Divide the noodles among four deep serving bowls, top with the mince mixture, green parts of the spring onions and garnishes and serve.

SERVES 4

500 g (1 lb 2 oz) Shanghai noodles
  or medium thick wheat noodles

SAUCE
3 tablespoons light tahini
3 tablespoons Maggi seasoning
  sauce or light soy sauce
2 teaspoons rice vinegar
2 teaspoons caster (superfine) sugar
½ teaspoon Chinese five spice
1 teaspoon toasted and ground
  Sichuan peppercorns
125 ml (4 fl oz/½ cup) Sichuan chilli
  oil (page 164)
2 garlic cloves, minced
125 ml (4 fl oz/½ cup) boiling water

MINCE MIXTURE
2 tablespoons vegetable oil
3 cm (1¼ in) piece of ginger, peeled
  and grated
3 spring onions (scallions), thinly
  sliced, white and green parts
  separated
100 g (3½ oz) Sichuan pickled
  mustard greens or vegetable
  of your choice
1 garlic clove, minced
250 g (9 oz) veggie mince or soaked
  textured vegetable protein
2 teaspoons Chinese sweet bean
  paste or hoisin sauce
2 teaspoons shaoxing rice wine
1 teaspoon dark soy sauce

GARNISHES
1 Lebanese (short) cucumber,
  cut into sticks
2 bunches bok choy, blanched
  and refreshed
1 handful coriander (cilantro) leaves,
  roughly chopped (optional)
80 g (2¾ oz/½ cup) roasted and
  salted peanuts
1 tablespoon toasted sesame seeds

Vegan with bite

When you want all the joy of a full Mexican spread, but just can't even. This recipe is packed with all the flavours and textures we love about Mexican cuisine, without much effort at all.

SERVES 4–6

3 tablespoons extra-virgin olive oil
1 brown onion, finely chopped
½ red capsicum (bell pepper), seeded and diced
½ green capsicum (bell pepper), seeded and diced
3 garlic cloves, minced
450 g (1 lb) veggie mince or soaked textured vegetable protein
1 teaspoon chilli powder, or to taste
2 teaspoons ground cumin
2 teaspoons ground coriander
½ teaspoon ground cinnamon
1 teaspoon sweet paprika
1 teaspoon dried oregano
1 × 400 g (14 oz) tin diced tomatoes
300 g (10½ oz/1½ cups) long-grain rice
150 g (5½ oz/1 cup) frozen corn kernels
1 × 400 g (14 oz) tin black beans, drained and rinsed
625 ml (21 fl oz/2½ cups) beef stock
3 spring onions (scallions), sliced, plus extra to serve
250 g (9 oz) shredded cheese
sliced avocado, chopped coriander (cilantro) leaves and lime wedges, to serve

Heat the oil in a wide shallow saucepan over a medium heat. Add the onion, capsicums and a big pinch of salt and cook for 5 minutes, or until softened. Add the garlic and cook for another minute. Add the mince or textured vegetable protein and fry, breaking it up into small bits if using veggie mince. Add the ground spices and oregano and cook for 30 seconds, then stir through the diced tomatoes and cook over a medium–low heat for 5 minutes. Add the rice and stir to coat in the spiced tomato mixture, then add the corn and black beans.

Pour over the stock and stir to combine. Bring the mixture to the boil, then reduce the heat to the lowest setting and cook, covered, for 20–25 minutes, or until all the liquid has been absorbed.

Remove the lid and stir through the spring onion and half the cheese. Shake the pan to even out the rice, then sprinkle over the remaining cheese. Cover with the lid once again and leave for 1 minute to melt the cheese. Finish with the avocado, coriander and extra spring onion and serve with lime wedges. If you really want to go all out, add some corn chips and a drizzle of hot sauce.

When I say a dish is slutty, I mean it in the best way possible; it is a compliment of the highest order. These are the kinds of dishes we're told not to love because they are too generous, a little naughty and definitely over the top. In reality, they're everything you want, so enjoy them with reckless abandon. Korean rice sticks are a chewy, delightfully textural wonder that should be part of every vegan's repertoire. Add cheesy, salty and garlicky flavours and a secret nostalgic ingredient (hot dogs!) and you have one OTT dish you'll go back to again and again.

SERVES 4

500 g (1 lb 2 oz) Korean rice sticks
750 ml (25½ fl oz/3 cups) water
1 × 5 cm (2 in) piece of dried kombu
1½ tablespoons gochujang
   (Korean chilli paste)
1 tablespoon gochugaru
   (Korean chilli flakes)
1½ tablespoons light soy sauce
1 tablespoon fish sauce (optional)
1½ tablespoons caster (superfine)
   sugar
2 garlic cloves, minced
150 g (5½ oz) kimchi,
   roughly chopped
3 spring onions (scallions),
   cut into 5 cm lengths, plus extra
   sliced spring onion greens to serve
4 hot dogs, cooked and sliced
125 g (4½ oz) grated cheese

Soak the rice sticks in a bowl of cold water while you make the sauce.

Pour the water into a wide shallow saucepan and add the kombu. Bring to the boil over a high heat, then reduce the heat to medium and simmer for 5 minutes, or until the liquid has reduced to about 500 ml (17 fl oz/2 cups). Remove the kombu.

Add the gochujang, gochugaru, soy sauce, fish sauce (if using), sugar and garlic to the kombu stock and stir well to combine. Mix through the kimchi and spring onion, then bring up to a simmer and cook for 1 minute.

Throw the rice sticks into the sauce and stir well to coat, then reduce the heat to low. Add the sliced hot dogs and cook for 5 minutes, stirring often as the rice sticks tend to catch on the bottom of the pan.

Once the rice sticks are soft, cover the surface with grated cheese. More is more! Place a lid on the pan and cook for another minute. Turn off the heat and leave the dish to stand, covered, for another 2 minutes, or until the cheese is melty. Sprinkle with extra spring onion greens and serve.

Cheesy Korean hot dog and kimchi spicy rice sticks (tteokbokki)

South Indian coconut rice

Rice is rice, but when a rice dish is so good that it can easily be the star of the show it's definitely worth incorporating into your repertoire. Frozen grated coconut is the hero here, and you can find it in almost any Indian or South Asian grocer. Every vegan-friendly freezer should reserve space for some, it's that good.

Melt the butter in a heavy-based saucepan over a medium heat, add the spices and cook, stirring, for 1 minute. Add the ginger, chillies and grated coconut and cook for another minute. Pour in the rice and stir well to coat in the spices, then fry for 1 minute.

Add the coconut milk, water and salt and bring to the boil, then reduce the heat to low and simmer, covered, for 30–40 minutes, or until all the liquid has been absorbed. Remove from the heat and fluff the rice with a fork. Cover the pan with a tea towel (dish towel) and allow to stand for 5 minutes before serving.

SERVES 4–6

40 g (1½ oz) butter or ghee
½ teaspoon fenugreek seeds
3 whole cloves
1 star anise
3 black peppercorns
½ teaspoon cumin seeds
1 teaspoon minced ginger
2 small green chillies, split
 lengthways
50 g (1¾ oz) grated
 frozen coconut
300 g (10½ oz/1½ cups)
 basmati rice
1 × 400 ml (13½ fl oz) tin
 coconut milk
375 ml (12½ fl oz/1½ cups) water
1 teaspoon salt

When I tested this recipe (designed to serve four) I ate the lot. I wasn't even hungry, it was just so damned good. I'm issuing a warning because it could happen to you too. My advice? Make twice as much as you think you need.

SERVES 2, OR 4 AS PART OF A BANQUET

5 garlic cloves, minced
4–6 red bird's eye chillies, finely chopped
3 tablespoons vegetable oil
200 g (7 oz) snake (yard-long) beans or green beans, cut into 5 cm (2 in) lengths
2 tablespoons soy sauce
1 tablespoon mushroom oyster sauce
1 tablespoon fish sauce
100 ml (3½ fl oz) chicken or vegetable stock
2 teaspoons caster (superfine) sugar
1 tablespoon cornflour (cornstarch)
½ bunch Thai basil, leaves picked
steamed jasmine rice, to serve

CRISPY TOFU

1 × 450 g (1 lb) block extra-firm tofu
2 tablespoons vegetable oil
3 tablespoons cornflour (cornstarch)
½ teaspoon onion powder
½ teaspoon garlic powder
1 teaspoon salt

To prepare the crispy tofu, drain the tofu and cut lengthways through the centre so you end up with two long, thin pieces. Place between sheets of paper towel and weigh down with some food tins or similar. Allow the tofu to drain for 30 minutes or so. Once dry, cut it into 2 cm (¾ in) cubes.

Preheat the oven to 200°C (400°F) and line a baking tray with baking paper.

Place the tofu in a large bowl, pour over the oil and toss to coat. Scatter in the cornflour, onion and garlic powder, salt and some pepper and toss again, ensuring all the tofu is well coated. Spread it out in a single layer on the prepared tray and bake for 20 minutes, then turn the tofu cubes over and bake for another 15 minutes, or until golden and crispy.

While the tofu is baking, mix the minced garlic and chilli on your chopping board, then sprinkle over a big pinch of salt. Using the flat side of your knife, press down and repeatedly drag it across the garlic and chilli until you have a rough paste. This can also be done with a mortar and pestle, if preferred.

Heat the oil in a wok over a high heat. Once hot, add the garlic and chilli paste and quickly toss for 10–15 seconds, then throw in the crispy tofu and beans and toss to coat.

Stir in all the sauces, stock, sugar and cornflour and toss regularly for about 1 minute to coat and combine, then throw in the basil leaves. Toss one last time and serve with steamed rice.

Puttanesca

You all know what puttanesca means, right? The namesake saints of this dish are prostitutes and, as we all know, sex work is real work. Unlike this dish. Which only seems that way.

Fill a large saucepan with heavily salted water and bring to a rapid boil. Throw in the pasta and cook for 1 minute less than it says on the packet.

Meanwhile, heat the oil in a large frying pan over a medium heat, add the garlic, capers, olives, chilli and oregano and cook for about 1 minute until beginning to turn golden. Drop in the tomato and stir to combine. Add the fish sauce and stir through, then increase the heat to high and simmer rapidly, stirring often, for 20 minutes, or until the sauce had reduced slightly. Add the parsley and season with salt and pepper.

When the pasta is ready, use tongs or a slotted spoon to pull it straight from the pan and dump it into the sauce. You want to have a little of the cooking water going into your sauce so it's important not to drain. Quickly toss the pasta through the sauce – not only to combine, but also to help emulsify the sauce. Scatter over some parmesan (if using) and serve.

SERVES 4–6

500 g (1 lb 2 oz) dried spaghetti
80 ml (2½ fl oz/⅓ cup) extra-virgin olive oil
6 garlic cloves, sliced
3 tablespoons capers in brine, rinsed
40 g (1½ oz/⅓ cup) pitted black olives, whole or roughly chopped
1 heaped tablespoon Italian chilli paste or chilli flakes
1 teaspoon fresh or dried oregano
800 g (1 lb 12 oz) tomatoes, chopped or 2 × 400 g (14 oz) tins diced tomatoes
2 tablespoons fish sauce
1 handful chopped flat-leaf (Italian) parsley leaves
grated parmesan, to serve (optional)

If you love mushrooms, this dish is for you.

SERVES 4–6

60 g (2 oz) mixed dried Chinese
mushrooms, soaked in hot water
for 20 minutes until soft (I suggest
dried black fungus/wood ears,
shiitake and lion's mane)

3 tablespoons vegetable oil

4 cm (1½ in) piece of ginger, peeled
and finely julienned

2 garlic cloves, finely chopped

2 spring onions (scallions),
thinly sliced

1 teaspoon Sichuan peppercorns,
crushed

150 g (5½ oz) baby king mushrooms

100 ml (3½ fl oz) shaoxing rice wine

500 ml (17 fl oz/2 cups) chicken
or vegetable stock

2 tablespoons light soy sauce

2 tablespoons Sichuan chilli oil
(page 164)

1 piece of dried mandarin peel
(otherwise use fresh orange
or mandarin peel)

1 small cinnamon stick

2 star anise

500 g (1 lb 2 oz) cheung fun rice
noodles (available from Asian
grocers), cut into 5 cm (2 in)
lengths

1 handful chopped coriander
(cilantro) leaves

1 tablespoon sesame oil

Strain the soaked mushrooms into a bowl, reserving the liquid.
Trim any hard stems from the mushrooms and squeeze out the
excess water, then cut the larger ones into bite-sized pieces.
Set aside.

Heat the oil in a wok over a high heat, add the ginger, garlic and
spring onion and stir-fry for 15 seconds, then add the Sichuan
peppercorns and stir-fry until fragrant, about 10 seconds.

Add the baby king mushrooms and stir-fry for 1 minute, or until
they begin to soften slightly, then add the soaked mushrooms and
toss to combine.

Pour in the shaoxing wine and cook until the wine has reduced by
half, then add the stock, soy sauce, chilli oil, citrus peel, cinnamon
stick, star anise and 250 ml (8½ fl oz/1 cup) of the reserved soaking
liquid. Bring to the boil, then reduce the heat to medium and simmer
until the sauce has reduced by about half and thickened to a syrup.

While the sauce is reducing, place the cut noodles in a microwave-
safe container with a lid and sprinkle with a little water. Cover,
leaving one corner open, and microwave for 1–2 minutes to soften
the noodles. You could also do this in a steamer if preferred.

Add the softened noodles and coriander to the sauce and stir
through. Finish with the sesame oil and serve.

Decidedly different from Indian curries, Sri Lankan curries have a distinctive flavour profile. This is just one version, but I hope it will inspire you enough to want to discover more.

SERVES 4–6

3 tablespoons vegetable oil,
 ghee or butter
1 teaspoon fenugreek seeds
20 curry leaves
2 brown onions, roughly chopped
6 garlic cloves
1 long red chilli
6 cm (2½ in) piece of ginger, peeled
 and roughly chopped
2 teaspoons ground cumin
1 teaspoon ground turmeric
1 tablespoon ground coriander
1 teaspoon chilli powder
2 teaspoons sweet paprika
1 teaspoon fennel seeds
2 teaspoons salt
3 tablespoons white vinegar
2 large potatoes, peeled and
 cut into large dice
180 g (6½ oz) button mushrooms
200 g (7 oz/1 cup) diced tomato
 (tinned or fresh)
1 lemongrass stem, bruised
6 black cardamom pods, bruised
1 cinnamon stick
375 ml (12½ fl oz/1½ cups) water
1 bunch English spinach,
 roughly chopped
250 ml (8½ fl oz/1 cup)
 coconut milk
80 g (2¾ oz/½ cup) frozen peas
1 handful coriander (cilantro) leaves
 (optional)
basmati rice, to serve

Warm the oil in a large heavy-based saucepan over a medium heat, add the fenugreek seeds and curry leaves and cook until they begin to colour.

Place the onion, garlic, chilli and ginger in a blender and blitz to a purée. Pour into the pan, reduce the heat to low and cook, stirring, for 10 minutes, or until slightly golden.

Add the ground spices, fennel seeds and salt and cook for 1 minute, then stir in the vinegar. Drop in the potato and mushrooms and stir to coat in the spice mix. Add the tomato, lemongrass, cardamom and cinnamon stick, season with pepper, add the water and stir well. Cover and cook for 20 minutes, stirring often.

Remove the lid and stir through the spinach, coconut milk and peas. Cook, uncovered, for another 5 minutes, or until the potato is tender. Garnish with coriander (if using) and serve with rice.

Mapo tofu

This is one of my all-time favourite things to eat.
As a meat eater, I am confident that this version is
as satisfying and delicious as one containing meat.
If you want to convince the meat eater in your life that
food can be just as good without it, or you're looking
to reduce the amount of meat you eat, this recipe is
a fantastic place to start.

Drain the tofu and cut into 2 cm (¾ in) cubes. Carefully place in a bowl and cover with boiling water and a big pinch of salt. Allow to sit while you proceed with the recipe.

Heat the oil in a wok over a high heat, add the mince or textured vegetable protein and fry for a minute, breaking it up into small bits if using veggie mince. Add the ginger, garlic and spring onion and stir-fry for a minute or so until the ginger and garlic are slightly golden. Throw in the fungus and toss to combine.

Add the doubanjiang and douchi and stir-fry for 30 seconds, making sure everything is evenly coated, then deglaze with the shaoxing wine. Pour in the stock and soy sauce, add the Sichuan pepper and bring to the boil, then reduce to a simmer.

Drain the tofu, then very carefully slide it into the wok and gently stir. Allow to simmer over a low heat for 10 minutes, then stir in the cornflour slurry and cook until thickened, about 3 minutes. Add the coriander and Sichuan oil and stir, then pour into a serving dish and serve.

SERVES 4–6

500 g (1 lb 2 oz) firm silken tofu
  (momen is my favourite)
boiling water, to cover
3 tablespoons vegetable oil
200 g (7 oz) veggie mince or soaked
  textured vegetable protein
6 cm (2½ in) piece of ginger, peeled
  and cut into fine matchsticks
4 garlic cloves, minced
3 spring onions (scallions), sliced
25 g (1 oz) dried black fungus (wood
  ears), soaked and sliced into strips
2 tablespoons doubanjiang (spicy
  fermented broad bean paste)
1 tablespoon douchi (fermented
  black bean paste)
2 tablespoons shaoxing rice wine
600 ml (20½ fl oz) chicken or
  vegetable stock
2 tablespoons light soy sauce
1 tablespoon Sichuan peppercorns,
  toasted and coarsely ground
2 tablespoons cornflour (cornstarch)
  blended with 80 ml (2½ fl oz/
  ⅓ cup) cold water
1 handful chopped coriander
  (cilantro) leaves
3 tablespoons Sichuan chilli oil
  (page 164)

I'm still not 100 per cent sure whether this is legitimately a Chinese dish, but one thing I do know is that my Australian nan knows how to make it. While my version is definitely more faithful to real Chinese flavours, there is something quite charming about westernised versions of Chinese cuisine. As a bonus, it'll be ready in less time than it takes to order home delivery.

SERVES 4

3 tablespoons vegetable oil, plus extra if needed

400 g (14 oz) chow mein noodles, cooked according to the packet instructions, drained well

300 g (10½ oz) veggie mince or soaked textured vegetable protein

2 tablespoons grated ginger

4 garlic cloves, minced

1 green chilli, sliced (optional)

3 spring onions (scallions), white parts only, sliced

1 teaspoon curry powder

1 small carrot, peeled and thinly sliced on the diagonal

200 g (7 oz) Chinese cabbage (wombok), roughly chopped

2 teaspoons cornflour (cornstarch) blended with 3 tablespoons cold water

SAUCE

80 ml (2½ fl oz/⅓ cup) oyster sauce

3 tablespoons shaoxing rice wine

2 tablespoons Maggi seasoning sauce or light soy sauce

1 tablespoon sesame oil

½ chicken stock cube or ½ teaspoon stock powder

1 teaspoon caster (superfine) sugar (optional)

200 ml (7 fl oz) water

Set a wok over a high heat for 2 minutes, then add a little oil and heat for 30 seconds. Divide the noodles into four bundles, then, working with one bundle at a time, place in the bottom of the wok and shape into a thin disc, adding a splash more oil for each bundle. Fry until crispy and golden, then flip and repeat on the other side. Remove and drain on paper towel. Repeat with the remaining noodles, then set aside.

If the wok still has some oil remaining, leave it in. If it's dry, add an extra splash and heat until smoking hot. Throw in the mince or textured vegetable protein and stir-fry for 1 minute, breaking it up into small bits if using veggie mince, then add the ginger, garlic, chilli (if using), white part of the spring onions and the curry powder and quickly stir-fry, making sure everything is evenly distributed. Add the carrot and cabbage and a splash of water to create a little steam, then cook for 2 minutes, or until the cabbage has wilted slightly.

To make the sauce, combine all the ingredients in a jar or small bowl. Pour into the wok and toss well, then bring to the boil and cook for 1 minute. Add the cornflour slurry, mix well and cook for a final 30 seconds, or until the sauce has thickened.

To serve, place the crispy noodle discs in shallow bowls and spoon over the chow mein mixture.

South Indian chickpea and silverbeet curry

Creamy, hearty, warming – all the things you want in a comfort dish. In essence, this curry is a hug in a bowl.

Place the onion, green chillies, ginger, garlic and tomato in a high-powered blender and blend to a rough purée.

Warm the oil in a heavy-based saucepan over a medium heat. Add the purée, along with the curry leaves and salt, and cook for 3 minutes, or until it looks a little dry. Add the turmeric, chilli powder, ground coriander, fennel seeds and garam masala and cook for 1 minute, stirring well.

Pour in the coconut milk and water and stir to combine, then add the chickpeas. Reduce the heat to low and simmer for 30 minutes, stirring often. Add the shredded greens and chopped coriander and stir to combine, then simmer for a further 15 minutes. Taste and season with salt and pepper if needed, then serve.

SERVES 4–6

1 red onion, roughly chopped

3 small green chillies

3 cm (1¼ in) piece of ginger, peeled and minced

3 garlic cloves, minced

1 tomato, diced

3 tablespoons coconut or vegetable oil

2 sprigs curry leaves, leaves picked

1 teaspoon salt

½ teaspoon ground turmeric

2 teaspoons chilli powder

1 tablespoon ground coriander

1 teaspoon fennel seeds, ground

2 teaspoons garam masala

1 × 400 ml (13½ fl oz) tin coconut milk

250 ml (8½ fl oz/1 cup) water

600 g (1 lb 5 oz) cooked chickpeas (tinned are fine)

½ bunch silverbeet (Swiss chard) or other greens, shredded

1 handful chopped coriander (cilantro) leaves

Indian and vegan food go hand in hand in a cliché world, but while this dish is traditionally made with cheese, chances are you won't notice its absence in this rendition.

SERVES 4–6

2 red onions, roughly chopped

6 cm (2½ in) piece of ginger, peeled and roughly chopped

2 green chillies, roughly chopped (seeds removed for less heat)

2 garlic cloves, smashed

750 g (1 lb 11 oz) frozen spinach, thawed, squeezed to remove excess moisture

375 ml (12½ fl oz/1½ cups) water, plus extra if needed

60 g (2 oz) butter

1 bay leaf

1 cinnamon stick

10 black peppercorns

1 teaspoon salt

1 tablespoon ground cumin

500 g (1 lb 2 oz) firm tofu (the harder the better)

1 teaspoon garam masala

125 g (4½ oz/½ cup) coconut yoghurt

Place the onion, ginger, chilli, garlic, half the spinach and 125 ml (4 fl oz/½ cup) water in a blender and blitz to a smooth paste.

Melt the butter in a large saucepan over a medium heat, add the bay leaf, cinnamon stick and peppercorns and cook until they start sizzling. Add the paste and salt and cook, stirring, for 2 minutes, or until the mixture becomes richer and darker in colour. Reduce the heat to low.

Blend the remaining spinach with 125 ml (4 fl oz/½ cup) water to a smooth paste. Add to the pan along with the cumin and stir well. Add the tofu and the remaining 125 ml (4 fl oz/½ cup) water and stir well to combine. Cover and cook for 20 minutes, stirring often to make sure the curry doesn't stick. Feel free to add a bit more water if you think it's becoming too thick.

Remove the lid and stir in the garam masala and yoghurt. Season with salt and pepper and cook for a further 5 minutes, then serve.

A whole roasted anything is often the crown jewel on the dinner table. Forget chicken – this is more impressive than that, and proof that vegan food can stand tall as the king on any dining table.

SERVES 4–6

1 large cauliflower head
extra-virgin olive oil, for drizzling

MARINADE
250 g (9 oz/1 cup) plain yoghurt
2 tablespoons tandoori spice blend
  (available from supermarkets
  or spice shops)
1 teaspoon salt
1 teaspoon grated ginger
1 garlic clove, grated
1 teaspoon tomato paste
  (concentrated purée)
1 teaspoon harissa paste (optional)
juice of ½ lemon

SPICED BUTTER
80 g (2¾ oz) butter or ghee
1 teaspoon black mustard seeds
1 teaspoon garam masala
2 sprigs curry leaves, leaves picked
1 teaspoon salt flakes

Preheat the oven to 170°C (340°F).

To make the marinade, combine all the ingredients in a bowl and season with pepper.

Place a rack over a baking tray that is at least 1 cm (½ in) deep, then sit the cauliflower on it. Liberally brush the marinade over the cauliflower, then drizzle with oil. Transfer to the oven, and carefully pour hot water into the baking tray (this will help steam the cauliflower while it roasts). Cook for 30 minutes, then baste the cauliflower with more marinade and roast for another 15 minutes.

Give it a final baste with the rest of the marinade, then turn up the oven to its highest setting (mine goes to 220°C/430°F). Roast for 15 minutes, or until the crust begins to turn very dark, almost black in some spots. Remove from the oven and place on a serving dish.

To make the spiced butter, melt the butter in a small frying pan over a medium heat. Add the mustard seeds and garam masala and fry until the mustard seeds begin to pop, then drop in the curry leaves and salt. WARNING: the leaves will spit! Fry for about 20 seconds, then pour over the cauliflower. READY TO SMASH.

This dish is simple, but it requires a bit of technique to nail. I promise it will be worth it though. If you're unfamiliar with this American classic, it's more pie than pizza, and the pride of Chicago for good reason.

Place the flour, polenta, salt, sugar and yeast in the bowl of an electric mixer fitted with the dough hook. Pour in the warm water and melted butter and mix on low speed to bring the ingredients together. Turn up the speed to somewhere between low and medium and knead the dough for 5 minutes, or until it is smooth and elastic.

Remove the dough from the mixer and shape into a smooth ball. Oil a large bowl with olive oil and drop in the dough. Coat the top of the dough with a little extra oil, then cover with a tea towel (dish towel) and leave to prove in a warm place for 1–2 hours, or until doubled in size.

Give the dough a little punch to remove the air, then place it on a floured bench. Roughly shape the dough into a rectangle, then roll out to 30 cm × 20 cm (12 in × 8 in).

Dot the cold butter over the dough, then spread evenly to cover the surface. Fold the dough from left to right at least five times to create layers, then shape it into a ball. Put it back in the bowl, cover and prove in the fridge for another hour to firm up the butter.

Preheat the oven to 200°C (400°F), along with a pizza stone or baking tray (this will help to cook the base before the top burns). Spray a 25 cm (10 in) springform cake tin with non-stick spray, or brush with olive oil.

Turn out the dough onto a floured bench and roll into a circle about 1.5 cm (½ in) thick. You want the dough to be roughly 5 cm (2 in) larger than your cake tin to allow for the high edges.

Carefully place the dough in the cake tin and press with your fist right into the edge, then press the dough against the side, forming a high crust.

To build your pie, start by evenly covering the base with shredded mozzarella. Top with the pizza sauce and finish with a layer of parmesan. Drizzle a little extra-virgin olive oil over the pie and bake for 20–30 minutes, or until golden. Allow to cool in the tin for 5 minutes before removing and slicing. If you are including any of the optional toppings, add them after the mozzarella layer.

NOTE
If you are including any of the optional toppings, it's best to cook them before adding them to your pizza pie to avoid excess liquid.

SERVES 4–6

270 g (9½ oz) plain (all-purpose) flour
3 tablespoons fine polenta
1 heaped teaspoon salt
2 teaspoons caster (superfine) sugar
1 heaped teaspoon dried instant yeast
125 ml (4 fl oz/½ cup) warm water
40 g (1½ oz) butter, melted, plus 40 g (1½ oz) cold butter
olive oil, for oiling and coating
non-stick cooking spray
300 g (10½ oz/2 cups) shredded mozzarella
250 ml (8½ fl oz/1 cup) Pizza sauce (page 163)
50 g (1¾ oz/½ cup) grated parmesan
extra-virgin olive oil, for drizzling

OPTIONAL TOPPINGS
basil leaves
sausage or salami
mushrooms
sliced onion
sliced capsicum (bell pepper)

Swedish meatballs

There really is something to be said for ugly delicious food. And Swedish meatballs are arguably at the pinnacle of ugly delicious, with beige sauce on top of brown meatballs and precious little else. What makes this dish, in many ways, is dill. I reckon it's one of the world's most underrated herbs, and it adds a freshness and dimension of flavour you can't really replicate with anything else.

The beauty of this recipe is the meatball base. Once you nail the technique, feel free to change the flavour profile to suit a bunch of other recipes; from spaghetti meatballs, to curries and stews, these meatballs are worth nailing.

Heat the olive oil in a small frying pan over a medium heat. Add the onion and a pinch of salt and cook, stirring, for a few minutes until softened. Add the garlic and caraway seeds and cook for another minute. Remove from the heat and set aside.

In a bowl, mix the mince, tofu, paprika, allspice, potato starch, salt and some pepper until well combined. With wet hands, form the mixture into meatballs the size of ping-pong balls.

To cook, you can either shallow-fry the meatballs in a frying pan or deep-fry them. Pan-frying will yield flatter meatballs, while deep-fried meatballs will be perfectly round.

To shallow-fry, heat 3 tablespoons vegetable oil in a frying pan over a medium heat and cook the meatballs for about 2 minutes each side, or until golden brown. You may need to cook them in batches to avoid overcrowding the pan.

To deep-fry, heat the vegetable oil in a heavy-based saucepan until it reaches 160°C (320°F) on a thermometer (or test by dropping in a small amount of meatball mix – it should start bubbling immediately). Deep-fry in batches until golden brown.

Remove the cooked meatballs with a slotted spoon and drain on paper towel while you prepare the sauce.

To make the sauce, melt the butter in a large frying pan over a medium heat, add the onion and caraway seeds and cook until slightly golden. Add the garlic and cook for another minute.

Sprinkle over the flour and cook, stirring, for 2 minutes until it starts to turn slightly golden. Slowly add the stock, stirring constantly to avoid any lumps. Add the vodka (if using) and whisk in the cream cheese or sour cream.

Add the meatballs to the sauce and cook over a low heat for about 5 minutes, stirring well to ensure the meatballs are evenly coated. Check the seasoning and add extra salt and pepper as needed, then stir through the dill and serve. This is great with mash and green beans or your favourite starch.

NOTE

If the sauce thickens too much after you have added the meatballs, add a splash of water.

SERVES 4–6

2 tablespoons olive oil
½ brown onion, finely diced
2 garlic cloves, minced
1 teaspoon caraway seeds
400 g (14 oz) fresh veggie mince (or use sausage, removed from casings)
100 g (3½ oz) medium/firm tofu, crumbled
2 teaspoons sweet paprika
½ teaspoon ground allspice
2 tablespoons potato starch
1 teaspoon salt
vegetable oil, for frying

SAUCE
40 g (1½ oz) butter
½ brown onion, finely chopped
1 teaspoon caraway seeds
2 garlic cloves, minced
2 tablespoons plain (all-purpose) flour
500 ml (17 fl oz/2 cups) beef stock
2 tablespoons vodka (optional)
2 tablespoons cream cheese or sour cream
1 very large handful dill, roughly chopped

DESSERTS

AND BAKED GOODS
YOU WILL LOVE

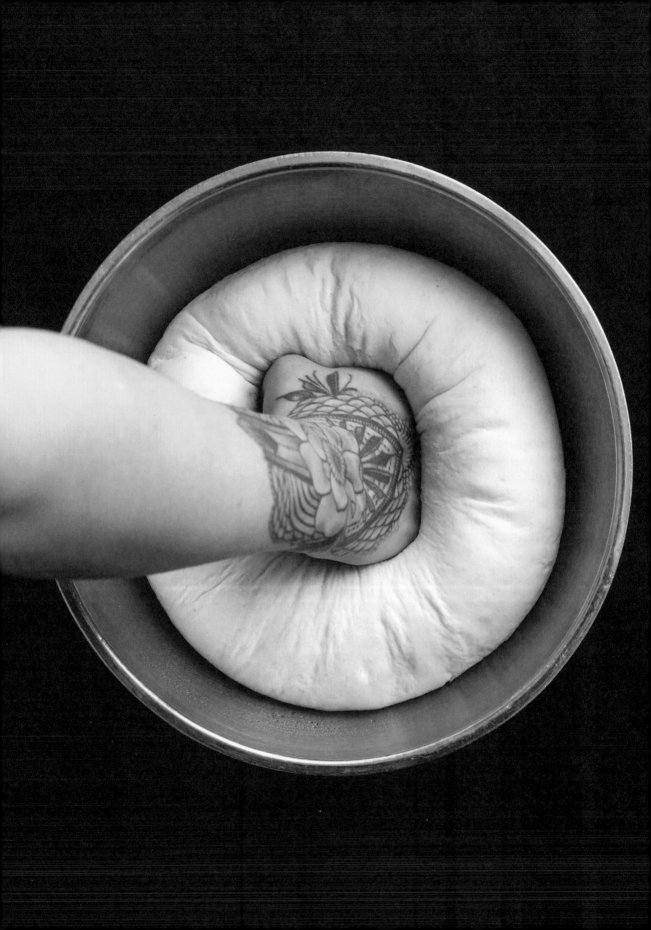

For someone who isn't generally a fan of desserts, it's ironic that I've become known for them. My approach to sweet dishes is to introduce savoury elements, which gives a more balanced result. Whether it's a pinch of salt or incorporating a savoury spice blend such as garam masala, this little tip can be a game changer. Balance in all things, right?

If you like apple pie and Mai Tais, this is the dessert for you.

SERVES 4–6

225 g (8 oz/1½ cups) plain
 (all-purpose) flour
2 teaspoons baking powder
2 tablespoons brown sugar
½ teaspoon salt
1 teaspoon mixed spice
½ teaspoon ground ginger
½ teaspoon Vegg (vegan egg yolk)
1 tablespoon No Egg
3 tablespoons cold water
170 ml (5½ fl oz/⅔ cup) milk
40 g (1½ oz) butter, melted
1 teaspoon vanilla extract
3 large apples (about 400 g/14 oz),
 peeled and cut into 1 cm (½ in)
 cubes
vegetable oil, for shallow-frying
salt flakes, for sprinkling

GLAZE

250 g (9 oz/2 cups) icing
 (confectioners') sugar
2 tablespoons spiced rum
2 tablespoons milk
½ teaspoon mixed spice
1 teaspoon vanilla extract

Sift the flour and baking powder into a large mixing bowl and stir in the brown sugar, salt, mixed spice and ginger.

Grab a smaller bowl and whisk together the Vegg, No Egg and water. Add the milk, melted butter and vanilla and whisk to combine. Pour into the flour mixture and stir until just combined, then fold through the apple.

Pour oil into a large frying pan to a depth of 7 cm (2¾ in) and heat over a medium–high heat to about 170°C (340°F), or until a cube of bread browns in 20 seconds. Using two spoons, drop heaped tablespoons of the mixture into the oil and fry for 3–4 minutes, turning often, until golden. Remove with a slotted spoon and drain on paper towel. Depending on the size of your pan you will probably have to cook them in a few batches.

To make the glaze, sift the icing sugar into a mixing bowl, then whisk in the remaining ingredients.

Line a tray or chopping board with baking paper and place a wire rack on top.

While the fritters are still warm, dip them into the glaze and roll around to coat evenly. Place the fritters on the rack and allow the excess glaze to drip off. Finish with a small pinch of salt flakes and leave for 10 minutes for the glaze to set, then serve warm (or at least within 24 hours).

Yes, it's called sticky fig pudding (swapping out dates for figs = revelation), but the secret to this dish is prunes. I know. Who would have thought that the laxative of the fruit world could elevate a dessert you thought was already perfect? The savoury spice mix garam masala balances out the sometimes sickly-sweet quality of this dish. A total crowd pleaser.

SERVES 4–6

180 g (6½ oz) dried figs,
  roughly chopped
100 g (3½ oz) pitted soft prunes,
  roughly chopped
1 teaspoon bicarbonate of soda
  (baking soda)
250 ml (8½ fl oz/1 cup)
  boiling water
120 g (4½ oz) unsalted butter,
  softened
3 tablespoons brown sugar
½ teaspoon Vegg (vegan egg yolk)
1 tablespoon No Egg
3 tablespoons cold water
185 g (6½ oz/1¼ cups) plain
  (all-purpose) flour
1½ teaspoons baking powder
½ teaspoon garam masala
½ teaspoon salt
vanilla ice cream, to serve

BUTTERSCOTCH SAUCE
200 g (7 oz) brown sugar
300 g (10½ oz) cream cheese
½ teaspoon vanilla paste or extract
80 g (2¾ oz) butter
½ teaspoon salt

Preheat the oven to 170°C (340°F). Grease and line a pudding basin (mould) or a 20 cm (8 in) springform cake tin.

Place the figs and prunes in a heatproof bowl and sprinkle over the bicarbonate of soda. Pour over the boiling water and leave to soften for 10 minutes, then mash with a potato masher or fork until fairly smooth.

Place the butter and sugar in a mixing bowl and beat with a wooden spoon until smooth and well combined.

Whisk together the Vegg, No Egg and cold water, then add to the butter mixture and beat through. It may look slightly curdled but that's totally fine. Sift in the flour, baking powder, garam masala and salt and mix until incorporated. Pour in the date and prune mixture and stir until well combined.

Pour the batter into the prepared basin or tin and smooth the surface. Bake for 35 minutes if you are using a springform tin, or about an hour if using a pudding basin, until a skewer inserted in the centre comes out clean.

Meanwhile, to make the butterscotch sauce, place all the ingredients in a saucepan over a medium heat and stir until the butter has melted. Bring to a simmer and cook for 2 minutes, stirring once, then remove from the heat.

Remove the pudding from the oven and poke holes all over the surface with a skewer. Pour over 125 ml (4 fl oz/½ cup) of the butterscotch sauce and leave to soak for 10 minutes. Serve with ice cream and the remaining sauce in a jug so people can add more if they like.

Forget cut, colour and clarity, these are the three Cs you need to know about. Coffee and chocolate are an established match made in heaven, but the added layer of fragrant savoury cardamom takes these cookies to a new level.

MAKES ABOUT 18

250 g (9 oz) dark chocolate, broken into pieces

1 teaspoon instant coffee powder mixed with 1 tablespoon boiling water

125 g (4½ oz) butter

1 teaspoon Vegg (vegan egg yolk)

1 tablespoon No Egg

80 ml (2½ fl oz/⅓ cup) cold water

100 g (3½ oz) caster (superfine) sugar

50 g (1¾ oz) brown sugar

1 teaspoon vanilla paste or extract

100 g (3½ oz/⅔ cup) plain (all-purpose) flour

1 teaspoon baking powder

1 teaspoon ground cardamom

½ teaspoon salt

100 g (3½ oz) dark choc chips

Preheat the oven to 160°C (320°F) and line two baking trays with baking paper.

Place the chocolate, coffee and butter in a heatproof bowl set over a saucepan of simmering water and melt until smooth and combined (don't let the bottom of the bowl touch the water). Remove the bowl and set aside to cool slightly.

Place the Vegg, No Egg and cold water in the bowl of an electric mixer fitted with a balloon whisk and whisk on high for about 1 minute. Add the sugars and beat on high for 3 minutes, or until fluffy. Swap the whisk for the paddle attachment, then pour in the vanilla and cooled chocolate mixture and mix on medium speed until well combined.

Sift the flour and baking powder over the chocolate mixture, add the cardamom and salt and mix on low until just combined. Quickly fold through the choc chips.

Drop tablespoons of batter onto the prepared trays, leaving at least 5 cm (2 in) between cookies to allow for spreading. (Depending on the size of your trays you may need to cook them in a couple of batches.) Bake for 10 minutes, then cool completely on the trays before removing. If you prefer a firmer cookie, add a few more minutes to the baking time.

El's rum, rye and sea salt cookies

The main reason I've been able to spend the time on this book is because I have one of the most passionate and talented pastry chefs, El Rosa, holding it down for me at the deli every day. It's only right that I include one of her recipes here because without her help, this book wouldn't exist.

This cookie recipe is one of her best and simplest ... no mean feat when it comes to asking a bona fide pastry goddess to share a recipe with home cooks! These cookies are my idea of a good time. They're soft and chewy, and the sweetness is offset by the rye, salt and rum. Perfect with a cup of tea.

Preheat the oven to 160°C (320°F) and line a large baking tray with baking paper.

Place the butter and sugar in the bowl of an electric mixer fitted with the paddle attachment and beat until pale. Beat in the vanilla.

In a separate bowl, combine the rum, No Egg and water, then add to the butter mixture.

Mix together the flours, cinnamon and bicarbonate of soda, then add to the butter mixture and mix until combined. Gently fold in the chocolate chunks.

Roll the dough into 12 even-sized balls. Place them on the prepared tray, allowing room for spreading, and gently press to flatten. Sprinkle a pinch of salt flakes on each cookie and bake for 8–10 minutes. Cool completely on the tray before removing.

MAKES 12

210 g (7½ oz) butter
190 g (6½ oz) brown sugar
1 teaspoon vanilla paste or extract
1½ tablespoons rum
1 teaspoon No Egg
1 tablespoon cold water
70 g (2½ oz) rye flour
200 g (7 oz/1⅓ cups) plain (all-purpose) flour
½ teaspoon ground cinnamon
½ teaspoon bicarbonate of soda (baking soda)
100 g (3½ oz) dark chocolate, chopped into chunks
salt flakes, for sprinkling

Apricot crumble cake

In my opinion, apricot is the queen of fruit for hot desserts. Admittedly, in their raw state, apricots aren't the most elegant of fruits, but they transform into something magical with the application of heat.

Preheat the oven to 170°C (340°F). Grease and line the base of a 20 cm (8 in) round cake tin.

Sift the flour, baking powder, salt and ground spices into a bowl. Mix in the sugar.

In a jug, whisk together the No Egg and water, then mix in the melted butter, milk and vanilla. Pour into the dry ingredients and stir until combined (the batter will be quite thick).

To make the crumble, place the flour, cinnamon and sugar in a small bowl, then rub in the butter with your fingertips to make a coarse crumble.

Pour the batter into the prepared tin and smooth the surface. Arrange the apricots on top, cut side up, then sprinkle over the crumble. Bake for 45–55 minutes, or until a skewer inserted in the centre comes out clean. Cool in the tin for 5 minutes, then carefully remove and cool completely on a wire rack. Finish with a light dusting of icing sugar if you like. Leftovers will keep in an airtight container for up to 3 days.

SERVES 8–12

225 g (8 oz/1½ cups) plain (all-purpose) flour
3 teaspoons baking powder
½ teaspoon salt
1 teaspoon ground cinnamon
½ teaspoon ground cardamom
115 g (4 oz/½ cup) caster (superfine) sugar
3 teaspoons No Egg
80 ml (2½ fl oz/⅓ cup) cold water
125 g (4½ oz) butter, melted
125 ml (4 fl oz/½ cup) milk
1 teaspoon vanilla paste or extract
1 × 825 g (1 lb 13 oz) tin apricot halves, drained (reserve the liquid for another use or reduce it with a little sugar and use as a syrup to drizzle over the cake)
icing (confectioners') sugar, for dusting (optional)

CRUMBLE
60 g (2 oz) plain (all-purpose) flour
1 teaspoon ground cinnamon
100 g (3½ oz) caster (superfine) sugar
55 g (2 oz) cold butter, cut into cubes

Chocolate cake is the last thing I would choose as a dessert, but using salt and olive oil transforms this one into a decidedly adult cake. Sour cherries add another element of balance, making it one chocolate cake that could prove the exception.

SERVES 8–12

500 ml (17 fl oz/2 cups) soy milk
2 teaspoons apple-cider vinegar
90 g (3 oz/¾ cup) cocoa powder
300 g (10½ oz/2 cups) plain
  (all-purpose) flour
1 teaspoon bicarbonate of soda
  (baking soda)
1 teaspoon baking powder
1½ teaspoons salt
460 g (1 lb/2 cups) caster
  (superfine) sugar
250 ml (8½ fl oz/1 cup) olive oil
200 g (7 oz) dark chocolate, melted
dark chocolate shavings and fresh
  cherries (optional), to garnish

QUICK CHERRY JAM
400 g (14 oz/2 cups) pitted sour
  cherries (jarred or fresh)
230 g (8 oz/1 cup) caster
  (superfine) sugar
1 teaspoon vanilla paste or extract
1 bay leaf
2 strips orange zest

COCONUT WHIP
1 × 400 ml (13½ fl oz) tin coconut
  cream, well chilled (see Notes)
60 g (2 oz/½ cup) icing
  (confectioners') sugar
2 teaspoons vanilla paste or extract

Preheat the oven to 170°C (340°F). Grease and line two 20 cm (8 in) springform cake tins.

In a small saucepan, whisk together the milk and vinegar. Add the cocoa and bring to the boil, whisking until it thickens slightly, then remove from the heat and set aside.

Sift the flour, bicarbonate of soda and baking powder into a mixing bowl, then stir in the salt and sugar.

Stir the olive oil through the melted chocolate, then whisk it into the warm milk. Add to the dry ingredients and stir well to combine.

Divide the batter evenly between the prepared tins and smooth the tops. Bake for 40 minutes, or until a skewer inserted in the centre comes out clean. Cool in the tin for 30 minutes, then carefully remove and cool completely on a wire rack. (You can cut the cooled cakes in half horizontally if you would like four cake layers.)

Meanwhile, to make the jam, place all the ingredients along with a pinch of salt in a small saucepan over a high heat. Bring to the boil, then reduce the heat to medium and simmer for 10 minutes, or until thickened. Remove the bay leaf and orange zest, then pour into a bowl and allow to cool.

For the coconut whip, take the tin of coconut cream out of the fridge, being careful not to shake it up. Gently open the tin and scoop the solid coconut cream into the bowl of an electric mixer fitted with a balloon whisk, leaving behind the coconut water that has separated at the bottom. (Save the coconut water for another use, such as your next curry or smoothie.) Add the icing sugar and vanilla and whip until light and fluffy. Store in the fridge until needed.

To assemble, top one layer of cake with just under half the coconut whip, building a lip around the edge, then drizzle over a layer of cherry jam. Top with the second cake and roughly mask with the remaining coconut whip, or just pipe it on the top. Drizzle with the remaining cherry jam, then use a peeler to finish with dark chocolate shavings and fresh cherries if you have some.

Any leftovers will store in an airtight container in the fridge for up to 3 days.

NOTES
It's important to use top-quality coconut cream made with only coconut extract and water (90% coconut extract content or more works the best). If you can plan ahead, chill it in the fridge for at least 24 hours before baking the cake.

If you don't have time to make the coconut whip, just use bought whipping cream.

An Australian classic that for some reason my Spanish father always made for us when we were growing up. I have no idea where he learned it, or why he made it, but I am very glad that he did.

SERVES 4–6

115 g (4 oz/½ cup firmly packed) brown sugar

500 ml (17 fl oz/2 cups) water

235 g (8½ oz/⅔ cup) golden syrup (see Note)

100 g (3½ oz) butter

225 g (8 oz/1½ cups) plain (all-purpose) flour

2 teaspoons baking powder

1 teaspoon vanilla paste or extract

185 ml (6 fl oz) milk

80 ml (2½ fl oz/⅓ cup) orange juice

cream or vanilla ice cream, to serve

Combine the brown sugar, water, 3 tablespoons golden syrup, 50 g (1¾ oz) of the butter and a pinch of salt in a large saucepan. Stir over a low heat until melted and combined, then remove from the heat.

Meanwhile, use your fingertips to rub the remaining butter into the flour and baking powder until it resembles fine breadcrumbs. Whisk the vanilla into the milk, then stir into the flour mixture until well combined.

Bring the sauce back up to the boil over a high heat. Carefully drop in heaped soup spoons of the dough and reduce the heat to low. Cover and simmer for 15–20 minutes, or until a skewer inserted into a dumpling comes out clean.

Combine the orange juice and remaining golden syrup in a small saucepan. Bring to the boil, then remove the syrup from the heat.

To serve, scoop the dumplings into bowls and spoon over the sauce. Finish with a drizzle of the warm orange syrup and serve with cream or ice cream.

NOTE

As far as golden syrup goes, if you're in a country that doesn't have it, look up the best equivalent ingredient. Just be aware that the substitution may not give the same result.

Lemon and blackberry self-saucing pudding

I love a science experiment recipe where you pour boiling water over cake batter and end up with oozy, lemony, completely delicious results. I suggest blackberries here but you can use whatever berries float your boat.

Preheat the oven to 180°C (350°F).

Sift the flour, baking powder and a pinch of salt into a medium bowl and stir through the sugar. Make a well in the centre, then pour in the milk, melted butter, lemon zest and vanilla and stir until just combined.

Grease a medium round high-sided baking dish with the extra butter, then pour in the batter, taking care to even out the surface. Push the blackberries into the batter.

To make the sauce, place the sugar, cornflour, lemon zest and basil in a small bowl and mix with your fingertips, then scatter over the batter. Heat the water and milk in the microwave or on the stove top until almost boiling, then pour in the lemon juice (it will curdle slightly). Pour evenly over the batter and bake for 40 minutes or until golden. Serve with cream or ice cream.

SERVES 4–6

150 g (5½ oz/1 cup) plain (all-purpose) flour
1½ teaspoons baking powder
115 g (4 oz/½ cup) caster (superfine) sugar
125 ml (4 fl oz/½ cup) milk
40 g (1½ oz) butter, melted, plus 2 teaspoons extra for greasing
finely grated zest of ½ lemon
1 teaspoon vanilla extract
65 g (2¼ oz/½ cup) fresh or frozen blackberries (if using frozen, don't let them thaw or they'll leave streaks in the batter)
cream or ice cream, to serve

SAUCE
115 g (4 oz/½ cup) caster (superfine) sugar
1 teaspoon cornflour (cornstarch)
finely grated zest of ½ lemon
5 basil leaves, finely chopped
185 ml (6 fl oz) water
125 ml (4 fl oz/½ cup) milk
80 ml (2½ fl oz/⅓ cup) lemon juice

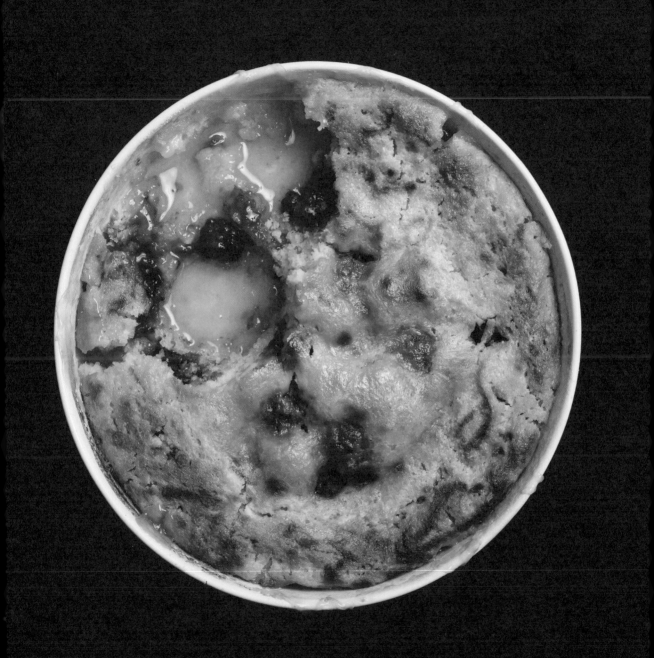

It's absolutely true that Australians stole pavlova from our New Zealand neighbours and made it our own. But regardless of where it came from, it isn't an Australian Christmas without one. If you like piña coladas, this one is for you.

SERVES 6

non-stick cooking spray
2 mangoes, flesh sliced into ribbons
pulp from 4 large passionfruit
¼ pineapple, peeled and
   very thinly sliced
mint leaves (optional)
coconut flakes, to garnish (optional)

MERINGUE
250 ml (8½ fl oz/1 cup) aquafaba
   (liquid drained from a tin of
   chickpeas), chilled in the freezer
   for 1 hour
230 g (8 oz/1 cup) caster
   (superfine) sugar
3 teaspoons vanilla paste or extract
1½ teaspoons xanthan gum
¾ teaspoon cream of tartar

LIME AND COCONUT WHIP
1 × 400 ml (13½ fl oz) tin coconut
   cream, well chilled (see Note)
40 g (1½ oz/⅓ cup) icing
   (confectioners') sugar
1 teaspoon vanilla paste or extract
finely grated zest of 1 lime

Preheat the oven to 130°C (250°F). Spray a baking tray with non-stick cooking spray and line with baking paper. This will help keep the paper in place when you spoon on the meringue mixture.

To make the meringue, pour the chilled aquafaba into the bowl of an electric mixer fitted with a balloon whisk. Add a pinch of salt and beat on high speed until soft peaks form. Reduce the speed to medium and gradually add the sugar. Once all the sugar is incorporated, add the vanilla, xanthan gum and cream of tartar, then continue beating until you have stiff peaks.

Scoop the meringue onto the prepared tray and, using a spatula, shape into a circle about 10 cm (4 in) high. Bake for 2½ hours, then turn off the heat and let the meringue cool in the oven with the door slightly ajar.

Meanwhile, make the lime and coconut whip. Take the tin of coconut cream out of the fridge, being careful not to shake it up. Gently open the tin and scoop the solid coconut cream into the bowl of an electric mixer fitted with a balloon whisk, leaving behind the coconut water that has separated at the bottom. (Save the water for another use, such as your next curry or smoothie.) Add the icing sugar, vanilla and lime zest and whip until light and fluffy. Store in the fridge until needed.

When the meringue has cooled completely, very carefully remove it from the tray and put it on a serving platter. Cover the top with a big pile of the coconut whip, then decorate with the mango, passionfruit, pineapple and mint and coconut (if using). Eat immediately.

NOTE
It's important to use top-quality coconut cream made with only coconut extract and water (90% coconut extract content or more works the best). If you can plan ahead, chill it in the fridge for at least 24 hours before making the pav.

Apple, strawberry and rhubarb pie

For those out there who battle with pastry, I offer this fail-safe dessert. While I am a chef who advocates cooking intuitively and according to feel, this is one instance where following the recipe will give you the best result. In non-vegan food, lard is the magic ingredient in golden flaky pastries. In a vegan recipe, vegetable shortening (*not* vegan butter) is the replacement you need to create the same texture and mouthfeel.

To make the pie crust, place the flour, icing sugar and salt in a food processor and pulse a few times until combined. Scatter over the butter and shortening and pulse again until the mixture resembles breadcrumbs. With the motor running on medium speed, slowly pour in the iced water, stopping as soon as the dough begins to form a ball. You may not use all the water.

Tip out the dough onto a floured surface and bring together with your hands until it forms a fairly smooth ball. Flatten into a disc, then wrap and chill for at least 30 minutes.

While the dough is chilling, prepare the filling. Combine all the ingredients in a large bowl and leave to macerate while the pastry is resting.

Preheat the oven to 200°C (400°F).

To assemble the pie, divide the dough into two pieces, making one piece slightly larger than the other. Roll out the larger piece on a floured surface to fit a 23 cm (9 in) deep pie dish, then line with the pastry, pushing it evenly into the base. Using a slotted spoon, scoop the filling into the pastry case, leaving behind any juices.

Brush the lip of the pie with a little milk. Roll out the remaining piece of pastry to fit the top of the pie and gently place over the fruit. Press the edges together with your thumbs, then trim off the excess pastry with a sharp knife. Create a pinched (crimped) effect around the edge of the pie by pressing the top and sides of the pastry together using your thumbs.

Brush the top of the pie with more milk, then sprinkle with raw sugar. Place the pie on a baking tray and bake for 15 minutes, then reduce the temperature to 170°C (340°F) and bake for another hour, or until golden. Allow to cool for at least 15 minutes before cutting.

SERVES 8–10

milk, for brushing
raw (demerara) sugar, for sprinkling

PIE CRUST
425 g (15 oz) plain (all-purpose) flour
50 g (1¾ oz) icing (confectioners') sugar
½ teaspoon salt
90 g (3 oz) cold butter, diced
150 g (5½ oz) cold vegetable shortening
100–120 ml (3½–4 fl oz) iced water

FILLING
250 g (9 oz) strawberries, hulled and halved
300 g (10½ oz) rhubarb, cut into 5 mm (¼ in) thick slices
300 g (10½ oz) peeled, diced apple
170 g (6 oz/¾ cup) caster (superfine) sugar
finely grated zest of 1 lemon
1 teaspoon vanilla paste or extract
1 teaspoon ground cinnamon
1 teaspoon chopped thyme
50 g (1¾ oz/⅓ cup) plain (all-purpose) flour
2 grinds of pepper

An excellent base recipe that you can customise with whatever you like. This vegan staple works well as a side, a wrap, or a dipping vehicle for almost any cuisine. To spice up the basic recipe, you can replace the yoghurt with coconut yoghurt for a slightly more fragrant take, topped with spiced butter.

MAKES 6–8

300 g (10½ oz/2 cups) plain (all-purpose) flour, or 150 g (5½ oz/1 cup) plain and 150 g (5½ oz/1 cup) wholemeal (whole-wheat) flour
300 g (10½ oz) of your favourite unsweetened plain yoghurt
1 teaspoon salt
½ teaspoon dried instant yeast
½ teaspoon caster (superfine) sugar

Base recipe

Place all the ingredients in the bowl of an electric mixer fitted with the dough hook and mix on medium–low speed until combined. Knead for 4–5 minutes, or until soft and elastic, then cover the bowl with a tea towel (dish towel) and prove until doubled in size, about 1 hour.

Knock back the dough, then divide it into six to eight even pieces. Roll out on a floured surface to a 3 mm (⅛ in) thickness. Don't worry about the shape, that's not important. It's all about how it tastes.

Heat a large chargrill pan or barbecue grill plate over a high heat until it's very hot. Add one flatbread and leave it alone for 2–3 minutes until it begins to puff up, then flip and cook on the other side for another 2–3 minutes. Cover to keep warm while you cook the rest.

300 g (10½ oz/2 cups) plain (all-purpose) flour, or 150 g (5½ oz/1 cup) plain and 150 g (5½ oz/1 cup) wholemeal (whole-wheat) flour
300 g (10½ oz) unsweetened coconut yoghurt
1 teaspoon salt
1 teaspoon za'atar
½ teaspoon dried instant yeast
½ teaspoon caster (superfine) sugar

SPICED BUTTER
100 g (3½ oz) butter
½ teaspoon grated ginger
1 garlic clove, grated
1 teaspoon masala spice mix (choose your favourite)
½ teaspoon black mustard seeds
1 sprig curry leaves (optional)

Coconut flatbread with spiced butter

Place the flour, yoghurt, salt, za'atar, yeast and sugar in the bowl of an electric mixer fitted with the dough hook. Make and rest the dough as described above.

To make the spiced butter, melt the butter in a small saucepan over a medium heat, add the remaining ingredients (except the curry leaves) and cook through for 30 seconds. Remove from the heat, add the curry leaves (if using) and set aside to infuse while you finish the flatbreads.

Roll out the dough and cook the flatbreads as described above. As you remove each piece from the pan, brush the top with the spiced butter. Serve warm.

What's better than pizza? Pizza folded in half and deep-fried of course! Vegan cheese is notorious for not having a good melt, but this problem is completely solved in this recipe. Folding the pastry to create a steam pocket gives the cheese everything it needs to make it great.

To make the dough, place the flour, semolina and salt in the bowl of an electric mixer fitted with the dough hook. Mix on low for 5 seconds to combine the ingredients.

In a jug or mixing bowl, whisk together the yeast, sugar, warm water and oil. Stand for about 5 minutes to allow the yeast to foam and become active. With the motor running on low speed, pour the yeast mixture into the dry ingredients and mix until almost absorbed, then increase the speed to medium and knead for 8 minutes, or until the dough is super soft and stretchy.

Coat a large mixing bowl with a little oil. Shape the dough roughly into a ball and place in the oiled bowl. Cover with a tea towel (dish towel) and allow to prove until doubled in size. Depending on the temperature of your kitchen, this can take anywhere between 45 minutes and 2 hours.

Once the dough has doubled in size, punch it! Knock out all the air and divide the dough into as many pieces as you like. Mini panzerotti or giant panzerotti? I'm not about to tell you how to live your life. Roll the dough pieces into balls, then cover with the tea towel and rest on a floured surface for about 15 minutes.

Roll out each ball on the floured surface to a disc about 3 mm (⅛ in) thick. Layer your fillings on one half of the circle, leaving a small border around the edge. Start with the pizza sauce, then the cheese, then whatever else you like. Fold the untopped dough over the filling and twist the edges together to seal. Place your completed panzerotti on a tray or flat surface sprinkled with semolina and cover with a tea towel while you make the remaining panzerotti and wait for the oil to heat up.

When you're nearly ready to cook the panzerotti, place a large saucepan filled with vegetable oil over a high heat (let common sense be your guide when it comes to the amount of oil you use – adjust according to the size you are making). Heat it to 170°C (340°F), or until a cube of bread browns in 20 seconds.

Carefully lower the panzerotti into the hot oil. How many you cook at once will depend on how big you've made them – just make sure you don't overcrowd the pan. Fry for a few minutes, then turn and cook until they are golden and crispy on both sides. Remove and drain on paper towel, sprinkle with salt flakes and EAT.

NOTE

The extras are your chance to make this your own. Try salami and basil, cooked mushrooms with thyme and garlic, roast pumpkin (squash) with rosemary, or anything else you can think of. The combinations are limitless.

SERVES 4–8

vegetable oil, for deep-frying
salt flakes, for sprinkling

DOUGH

700 g (1 lb 9 oz/4⅔ cups) plain (all-purpose) flour
300 g (10½ oz) semolina
1 tablespoon salt
7 g (¼ oz) dried instant yeast
1 tablespoon caster (superfine) sugar
700 ml (23½ fl oz) warm water (blood temperature)
2 tablespoons extra-virgin olive oil

FILLING

Pizza sauce (page 163) or your favourite tomato sugo
your choice of cheese (I like a combination of mozzarella and parmesan)
extras (see Note)

CREAM

CONDIMENTS RULE EVERYTHING AROUND ME:

DIPS, SAUCES AND SPREADS EVERY VEGAN NEEDS TO KNOW

The essentials. The things you need to make everything OK. No condiments, no life.
The end.

Smoky eggplant dip

It's always fun to set things on fire in the kitchen (when you mean to). This rich, smoky eggplant dish is great as a dip or spread and essential for any vegan mezze set-up.

Begin by roasting the eggplants over an open flame if possible as it will produce a smokier flavour. You want to cook them until they're black, collapsing and blistered all over. (If you have an induction or electric stove, cook them under a hot grill/broiler until you get the same result.) Once cooked, place the eggplants in a bowl, cover with a tea towel (dish towel) or plastic wrap and allow to cool for 20 minutes.

Once the eggplants are cool enough to handle, remove as much of the charred skin as possible and put the pulp in a fresh bowl, along with half of the smoky resting juices.

Now, while you are more than welcome to use a food processor for this next step, I personally find that mixing by hand gives you a more authentic texture. Add the tahini, garlic, lemon juice, cumin, paprika, salt, oil and hot sauce (if using), season with pepper and mash with a fork until well combined.

To serve, transfer the dip to a serving bowl, drizzle generously with extra oil and garnish with parsley and pomegranate molasses.

Pictured page 161

SERVES 4–6

2 medium eggplants (aubergines)
135 g (5 oz/½ cup) light tahini
4 garlic cloves, minced
juice of 2 lemons
1 teaspoon ground cumin
½ teaspoon smoked paprika
1 teaspoon salt
3 tablespoons extra-virgin olive oil, plus extra to serve
1 tablespoon hot sauce (optional)
flat-leaf (Italian) parsley leaves and pomegranate molasses, to garnish

In my opinion, my non-dairy version of this Greek favourite loses nothing of its true spirit in translation.

SERVES 4–6

2 large Lebanese (short) cucumbers, seeds removed and grated
500 g (1 lb 2 oz/2 cups) yoghurt (see Note)
3 tablespoons extra-virgin olive oil
1 tablespoon dried mint
1 small handful chopped dill
2 tablespoons lemon juice
2 garlic cloves, minced
½ teaspoon ground cumin
1 teaspoon salt flakes

Using your hands, scoop up the cucumber and squeeze out as much liquid as possible, then place in a medium mixing bowl. Add the remaining ingredients and mix well to combine.

Pictured page 160

NOTE
The reality is, vegan yoghurt is still not quite there in comparison to dairy yoghurt. While some brands may appear to be thick and creamy, they're not – they're just thickened with agar or something similar. If your favourite yoghurt is a little thin, I have a trick for you. Pour it into a nut milk bag, a piece of muslin (cheesecloth) or even a clean loose-weave kitchen wipe and hang it over a bowl to let the excess liquid drain out. It's the same method you use when making traditional labneh. After a few hours, you are left with beautifully thick yoghurt.

I know, vegans and hummus. But if you're going to do it, you might as well make it the best it can be, right?

Put everything (except the hot water or cooking liquid) in a blender, season generously with salt and pepper, and blend on high speed until smooth and well combined. Taste and adjust the seasoning if needed.

If you prefer a thinner hummus, slowly drizzle in some hot water or cooking liquid until you reach your perfect texture.

Pictured page 161

SERVES 4–6

650 g (1 lb 7 oz) cooked chickpeas (tinned is fine)
135 g (5 oz/½ cup) light tahini
125 ml (4 fl oz/½ cup) extra-virgin olive oil
4 garlic cloves, minced
1 tablespoon ground cumin
juice of 2 lemons
hot water or chickpea cooking liquid (optional)

OPTIONAL EXTRAS:
- 2 tablespoons ajvar (a spicy red pepper number from the Balkan region of the planet)
- a handful of your favourite soft herbs, like mint, flat-leaf (Italian) parsley or dill
- 4 chipotles in adobo (these come in a jar or tin and are a smoky, spicy flavour bomb)
- crispy chickpeas, deep-fried or roasted in the oven until crispy

Not the same as red sauce, but just as relevant for more than just pizza – you can use it as a base for stews, soups and pasta.

MAKES APPROX. 700 ML (23½ FL OZ)

3 tablespoons extra-virgin olive oil
20 g (¾ oz) butter
1 small brown onion, finely chopped
2 large garlic cloves, minced
½–1 teaspoon chilli flakes
375 ml (12½ fl oz/1½ cups) passata (puréed tomatoes)
1 × 400 g (14 oz) tin good-quality finely chopped tomatoes
1 teaspoon dried oregano
1 teaspoon caster (superfine) sugar (optional)

Warm the oil and butter in a medium saucepan over a medium heat, add the onion and a big pinch of salt and cook for a few minutes until softened. Throw in the garlic and chilli flakes and cook for another minute.

Add the passata and tinned tomatoes, then the oregano, a good pinch each of salt and pepper and the sugar (if you like a slightly sweeter sauce). Stir well to combine, then reduce the heat to low and cook for 30 minutes, stirring often.

Use the sauce straight away or store it for another time. To do this, let it cool completely, then portion it into small containers or zip-lock bags so you have pizza sauce ready to go whenever you need it. It will keep in the fridge for up to 5 days or in the freezer for a year!

Life without this holy grail of oils is meaningless.

Place the chilli flakes, Sichuan pepper, star anise, cinnamon stick, sesame seeds, fennel seeds and bay leaves in a large heatproof bowl and mix together.

Pour the oil into a saucepan, add the ginger and garlic and warm over a medium heat to 180°C (350°F). If you don't have a thermometer, you'll know the oil is ready when the garlic and ginger begin to turn a light golden colour around the edges.

Carefully pour the hot oil over the chilli mixture – it will bubble up slightly. Using a metal spoon, stir the oil through the chilli mixture to make sure everything is evenly cooked. Leave to infuse for 1 hour before removing the star anise, cinnamon stick, bay leaves, ginger and garlic.

Store the oil in a clean jar. It'll be fine on the bench for a few weeks, or in the fridge for a few months. Not that it will last that long.

**MAKES APPROX. 750 ML
(25½ FL OZ/3 CUPS)**

60 g (2 oz) chilli flakes

2 tablespoons Korean chilli flakes (or just add an extra 2 tablespoons normal chilli flakes)

1 teaspoon Sichuan peppercorns, ground

4 star anise

1 cinnamon stick, broken in half

50 g (1¾ oz/⅓ cup) toasted sesame seeds

1 teaspoon fennel seeds

2 bay leaves, crushed

625 ml (21 fl oz/2½ cups) vegetable oil

2 cm (¾ in) piece of ginger, peeled and thinly sliced

2 large garlic cloves, crushed

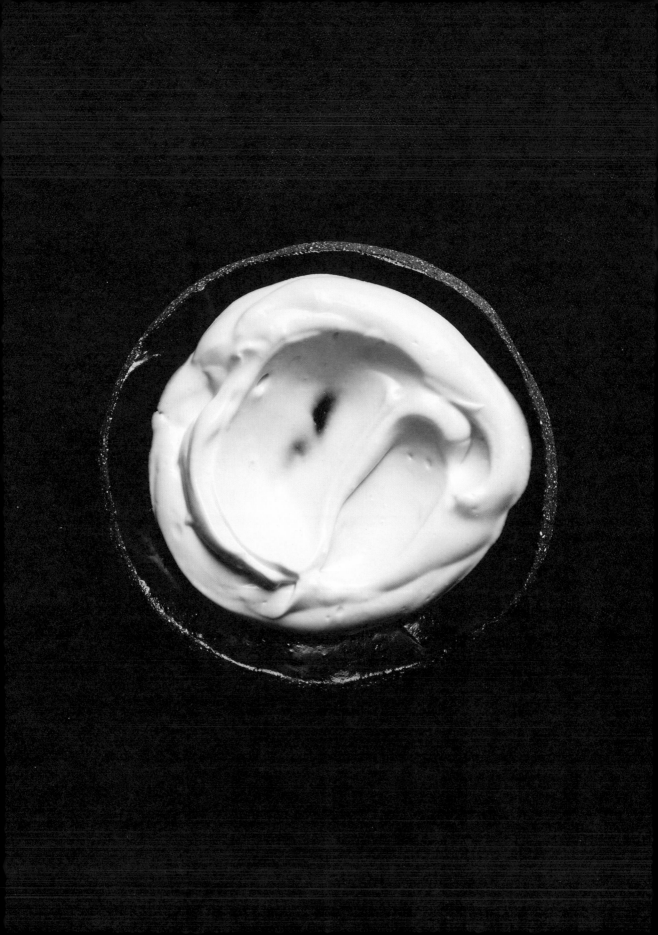

I love everything about mayo. Have this delight in your fridge at all times to make any salad, pasta or sandwich better than it would be without it.

**MAKES APPROX. 500 G
 (1 LB 2 OZ/2 CUPS)**

80 ml (2½ fl oz/⅓ cup)
  unsweetened soy milk
2 teaspoons apple-cider vinegar
2 teaspoons American mustard
½ teaspoon salt
1 teaspoon caster (superfine) sugar
250 ml (8½ fl oz/1 cup)
  vegetable oil
splash of hot water (optional)

Place the milk, vinegar, mustard, salt and sugar in the jug of a blender and blend until combined. Slowly drizzle in the oil with the motor running on medium speed. Check the consistency. If you prefer a thinner mayo (for a salad dressing, for example), thin it out with a little hot water with the blender running. Scoop into a clean jar and store in the fridge for up to a week.

TURNING TRASH INTO TREASURE

ZERO WASTE, MAXIMUM TASTE

No matter who you are – meat eater, vegan, or somewhere in between – we know that we all need to eat more sustainably and responsibly. Is there anything better than turning something you would otherwise throw away into something tasty that you love? Veganism isn't just about not eating animal products; it's about living in a way that is friendlier to the planet. This includes doing more with what we have and discarding less. For example, we are taught that the only valuable part of the carrot is the bottom bit, but did you know that the tops are actually delicious, and have a heap of applications aside from being the star of your compost? This chapter is here to change your mind about waste. From veggie tops, herb stalks and leftover wine (that exists?!) to apple peels and so many other things, here are a few recipes to turn your trash into treasure. You'll soon agree that nothing is actually trash if you know what to do with it.

Found a tired bag of carrots in the bottom of your fridge? This recipe is perfect for upcycling them into something delicious. Make a huge batch and freeze some for a rainy day.

Warm the vegetable oil in a large saucepan over a low heat, add the garlic, onion and salt and pepper and stir to combine. Increase the heat to medium and cook until the onion is translucent but hasn't taken on any colour. Add the carrot and cook for another 5 minutes.

Stir in the miso paste, then pour in enough stock to cover the veg. Bring to a simmer, then cover and cook for 25–30 minutes, or until the vegetables collapse under the pressure of a spoon.

Remove the pan from the heat, add the olive oil and blitz with a hand-held blender until smooth. Taste and adjust the seasoning if necessary, and serve with a drizzle of spring onion oil.

Pictured page 175

SERVES 4–6

3 tablespoons vegetable oil
3 garlic cloves, finely chopped
2 brown onions, roughly chopped
1 teaspoon salt
1 teaspoon white pepper
10 carrots, peeled, topped and
  tailed, then cut into chunks
2 tablespoons white miso paste
about 1.5 litres (51 fl oz/6 cups)
  chicken or vegetable stock
2½ tablespoons olive oil
Spring onion oil (page 179), to serve

Vegan with bite

Broaden your pesto horizon by turning leftover carrot tops into a tasty condiment. Use instead of basil and pine nut pesto with pasta, in dressings or as a spread. You can turn any leafy green into a delicious pesto using this recipe – try rocket, salad greens, leftover herbs, beetroot tops ... the sky's the limit!

MAKES APPROX. 250 G
(9 OZ/1½ CUPS)

2 bunches carrot tops (or any other green leafy veg you have lying around), well washed
1 handful basil leaves
finely grated zest of 1 orange
1 garlic clove, peeled
3 tablespoons grated parmesan
125 ml (4 fl oz/½ cup) extra-virgin olive oil
1 teaspoon salt

Blanch the carrot tops and/or other greens in boiling water for 30 seconds, then immediately refresh in cold water. Transfer to a blender, add the remaining ingredients, season with pepper and blitz. Done!

Pictured page 174

Citrus cordial

When life gives you lemons and you're sick of lemonade, here's what you can do with any leftover juice and peels. Citrus cordials are great to store in the fridge and make drinks with later. This recipe is from my friend Joe Jones, who is the best bartender I know, but these tips work just as well for home as they do at the bar.

Combine equal amounts of any citrus juice (there's often a surplus after a busy night at a bar, so it could help to make friends with your local bartender!) and granulated sugar – for example, 500 ml (17 fl oz/2 cups) lemon/lime juice and 500 g (1 lb 2 oz) sugar. Place in a large non-reactive container, add any remaining citrus peel and stir until combined and the sugar has completely dissolved. Cover and leave to sit at room temperature for at least 5 hours. Strain and store in a sterilised jar or bottle for up to 1 month.

You can always adjust the sweetness to suit your taste. For the adventurous, adding toasted spices to your cordial is a great idea. If you want to do this, toast 2 tablespoons whole spices in a dry frying pan over a medium–low heat until aromatic. Cool, then stir through the cordial and leave to infuse.

Grapefruit and cumin are a fantastic combination, as is lime and cardamom. A toasted cinnamon stick and a blistered bay leaf in your lemon cordial make for an exceptionally fun, no-fuss Tom Collins when paired with your favourite dry gin.

If you're planning a Sunday session with a specific drink in mind, I have thoughts about this too:

- Lime = stirred Gimlets
- Grapefruit = Palomas
- Lemon = Lynchburg Lemonades
- Orange = it doesn't work. Don't do it!

And of course it's most enjoyable in non-alcoholic drinks as well.

Another note on citrus: when you're done with drinks, pop the spent peels into a sterilised jar and top it with white vinegar. After two weeks, you have a non-toxic kitchen cleaner that works wonders.

Sweet berry wine!

I know, I know. Leftover wine? Is there such a thing? You can do lots with leftover wine, but the two best things are wine syrup and wine vinegar.

Wine syrup

Place a 1:1 ratio of wine to granulated sugar (for example, 100 ml/3½ fl oz wine to 100 g/3½ oz sugar) in a saucepan and stir over a medium heat until the sugar has dissolved. Allow to cool slightly, then store in a sterilised jar in the fridge. Try adding it to cocktails, or poaching fruit in it.

Wine vinegar

There are heaps of recipes out there that use vinegar containing 'the mother' to ferment wine, but the easiest way to make wine vinegar is to leave wine in the bottle, cover the top with some cheesecloth (muslin) or another breathable fabric (to prevent fruit flies), and let it naturally oxidise for 3–4 weeks. Once it's funky and fermenty, you can store it in the fridge and use it in salad dressings and vinaigrettes.

Spring onion oil

You could throw them in the bin, or use leftover spring onion tops to make this delicious, vibrant oil that's good with anything and everything.

MAKES APPROX. 300 ML (10 FL OZ)

leftover tops of 1–2 bunches spring onions (scallions)
leftovers of literally any dark green herb, such as
  coriander, flat-leaf (Italian) parsley or basil
300 ml (10 fl oz) neutral oil, like grapeseed or canola

Thoroughly wash the greens and pat them dry. This oil is best if there is no excess moisture so lay everything out on a tray and leave it in the fridge until properly dry. You'll end up with a better, more vibrant green oil this way. Roughly chop everything and throw it in a blender or food processor, add the oil and blitz to make a thick purée. It should look like a green smoothie … do NOT drink it!

Pour the purée into a saucepan and warm gently over a medium–low heat until the oil begins to separate from the pulp. The oil should reach a simmer, but not boil. Carefully pass the oil through a fine-mesh sieve and discard the pulp. Pour the oil into a sterilised jar or bottle, then immediately place in the freezer for 30 minutes to chill the oil and preserve the vibrant green colour. After 30 minutes, store the jar in the fridge.

Because the oil only keeps for a week or so, it's best made in small amounts and often rather than in huge batches. Use it to dress salads or freshly sliced tomatoes, or drizzle a teaspoon over mapo tofu, hummus or even your favourite soup just before serving. It's even great on plain pasta, seasoned with salt and parmesan.

Hainanese spring onion sauce

This recipe comes to you courtesy of my pal Melissa Leong. It's a great way of using up leftover spring onions (there are always some lying around). Chop off the roots and regrow them in your yard or even in a pot on your windowsill, then make this with the green bits.

SERVES 4

125 ml (4 fl oz/½ cup) vegetable oil
6 cm (2½ in) piece of ginger, peeled and
  coarsely grated
3–4 garlic cloves, finely chopped
½ bunch spring onions (scallions), finely chopped
white pepper
a few drops of sesame oil

Warm the vegetable oil in a small saucepan over a low heat.

Combine the ginger, garlic and spring onion in a small heatproof bowl.

Once the oil is hot, pour it over the spring onion mixture. Season with salt and pepper, then stir in the sesame oil. Pour into a sterilised jar and store in the fridge for up to a week (if it lasts that long).

Pangrattato

Celery salt

When I was growing up I had a friend whose mum would freeze bread. My mum wasn't a bread freezer, so it's something that stuck in my memory. Whenever you buy a beautiful loaf of bread and it passes its prime, pangrattato is the perfect thing to make (maybe with the exception of the Tomato and bread soup on page 61). In fact, you should never go to the shops to buy ingredients to make this – it is literally a trash-into-treasure situation. Simply blitz old bread, store it in the freezer and when you have enough, make this recipe. The quantities depend entirely on how much bread you have, so go with your gut and you'll find your own way.

You will need:

stale breadcrumbs
finely grated lemon zest
chilli flakes
garlic cloves, minced
olive oil
leftover herbs (oregano, rosemary and thyme work really well, but just use what you have)

Preheat the oven to 170°C (340°F).

Toss together all the ingredients and spread out evenly on a baking tray. Toast in the oven until golden, stirring occasionally so everything colours evenly, then turn the heat off and leave the crumbs in the oven to cool and dry out. When they're done I like to add a handful of parmesan, but you don't have to. Store in the fridge or freezer, then use it to top pasta and gratins, scatter over a Caesar salad instead of croutons, or simply add texture to almost any dish.

The dark green outer leaves of celery are bitter and tough and quite frankly have no place in salads or stocks. What they are great for, however, is celery salt: a condiment you can easily make yourself that will add a savoury, vegetal seasoning punch to everything from scrambled eggs to soups and stews.

Simply lay the dark green leaves on a lined baking tray and place in the oven on the lowest setting, with the door slightly ajar. Leave to dehydrate overnight. (You can also use a dehydrator if you have one.) When dry and cool, blitz them with a fistful of salt and store in a sterilised jar. Treat it like a stock seasoning and add a teaspoon to soups, stocks and stews.

Mushroom powder

Apple jam

Far from being mushroomy, this powdered wonder is a vegan MVP and adds a savoury umami punch to everything you cook. Porcini mushrooms can be really expensive, so for the vegan cook on a budget I recommend going to your local Asian grocer and finding a huge packet of dried sliced shiitake mushrooms – they're so cheap they're almost free. Then buy yourself a small packet of dried porcini mushrooms and blitz the whole lot together in blender. Throw a few teaspoons into almost every savoury dish you make.

Apple skins are high in pectin – the magical ingredient that makes jam, er, jammy! This is a really fun recipe to teach kids (little ones and big ones), perfectly highlighting the value of zero waste.

MAKES APPROX. 900G

cores and peels of 10–15 apples
about 920 g (2 lb/4 cups) caster (superfine) sugar
about 125 ml (4 fl oz/½ cup) lemon juice

Place the cores and peels in a large saucepan, cover with about 4 litres of water and bring to the boil over a high heat. Reduce the heat to medium and continue to boil until the water has reduced by half, then strain out the apple bits. Measure the liquid, and for every 250 ml (8½ fl oz/1 cup) of apple liquid, add 115 g (4 oz/½ cup) sugar and 1 tablespoon lemon juice. Bring this mixture to the boil, stirring regularly, until you have a gel-like consistency. Pour into sterilised jars and store at a cool room temperature or in the fridge. If stored properly, it should last months.

Index

Vegan with bite

Index

Vegan with bite

About the author

Acclaimed chef Shannon Martinez is an unlikely candidate to be the poster girl for plant-based dining. But she is, and she's unstoppable. Shannon is on a mission to change the way people perceive plant-based food and the way they eat it. In her case, it's coming from a different perspective: being a meat eater gives Shannon the insight to create tastes and textures that are unlike anything on the market today, dreaming up recipes that truly replicate meats, cheeses, and good old family favourites.

Over more than two decades of cooking in Melbourne kitchens, Shannon has developed a following among fans and peers alike for her out-of-the-box thinking and try-anything approach. She is the owner of Australia's two most prolific plant-based businesses, Smith & Daughters and Smith & Deli. As well, she is the co-author of two bestselling books, *Smith & Daughters: A Cookbook (That Happens To Be Vegan)* and *Smith & DELIcious: Food From Our Deli (That Happens To Be Vegan)*.

Thank you

I'd like to thank my family, Duncan, Mel, Nikki, Zian, Sam, Tamara, Joe, Lee, Vaughan, Ash and all my friends and staff for helping me during the most important and exciting time for myself and Smith & Daughters.

Published in 2020 by Hardie Grant Books,
an imprint of Hardie Grant Publishing

Hardie Grant Books (Melbourne)
Building 1, 658 Church Street
Richmond, Victoria 3121

Hardie Grant Books (London)
5th & 6th Floors
52–54 Southwark Street
London SE1 1UN

hardiegrantbooks.com

A catalogue record for this
book is available from the
National Library of Australia

Vegan With Bite
ISBN 978 1 74379 624 5

10 9 8 7 6 5 4 3 2 1

Publishing Director: Jane Willson
Project Editor: Anna Collett
Writer: Melissa Leong
Editor: Rachel Carter
Design Manager: Jessica Lowe
Designer: Vaughan Mossop
Photographer: Nikki To
Stylist: Lee Blaylock
Production Manager: Todd Rechner
Production Coordinator: Mietta Yans

Colour reproduction by Splitting Image Colour Studio
Printed in China by Leo Paper Products LTD.